My Crazy Deposition

B KUFFEL

Copyright © 2018 by B Kuffel

All rights reserved.
No part of this publication may be reproduced, stored in a retrieval system or transmitted, in any form or by any means—electronic, mechanical, photocopying, recording or otherwise—without prior written permission from the publisher, except for the inclusion of brief quotations in a review.

ISBN (Print): 978-1-7327228-1-1
ISBN (Ebook): 978-1-7327228-0-4

Interior Design by Booknook.biz.

DEDICATION

I would like to dedicate this book to my family and friends who have supported me throughout this process. I would like to thank my husband for always supporting me in going to court and standing up for what I believe in. I want to thank my kids for their understanding throughout this process. I want to thank my mom for the countless hours she helped me day and night. I want to thank my dad for always being there. I want to thank all my friends and the support that they have given me. This has been a very difficult and stressful process and without your support it would have been too much at times.

Acknowledgements

I would like to thank A. A. for all your help with editing and the support you have given me over the years. You are a wonderful young woman and I wish you the best always.

I would like to thank Kib Prestrige for your help with the book cover. Thank you so much for helping make this happen and I wish you the best always.

My Crazy Deposition

Here is the deposition I had to attend prior to court. The deposition was one of the worse experience of my life. Not only was it humiliating because of some of the questions, but the treatment from the opposing council inside the room was horrible at times. My deposition was so close to trial I was never able to see it in time to help me in my case. When I had the chance to read my deposition after court was over, I was even more upset. All the emotions of that day came right back to me. Presenting this deposition is not about the actual case, but about the process only.

I was there from 9:00 AM to about 4:20 PM, which included a couple of short breaks and a lunch. I think the amount of time a deposition is allowed to be held for is to extensive, 7 hours. A 7 hour deposition of you being asked questions (some questions over and over), sometimes in a hostile tone, wears on you mentally and physically. This process is very expensive, a cost that comes out of your own pocket for your attorney and possibly their fees if they file paper work that states if you don't win and over a certain amount you have to pay theirs.

When I read my deposition I was flabbergasted at how I had responded to some of the questions. I have had friends who had to go to depositions for various reasons. They said the same thing; they could not believe how they had answered some of the questions when they had read their depositions. They also felt that what you hear in your mind is not always what comes out in the answer, I attribute this to the stress you are feeling psychologically and physically. You need to remain focused, once your concentration drifts it effects your responses and they can use those against you. I found myself thinking back on the previous question and questioning myself on how I answered it. I know this affected some of my answers.

Two days before my deposition I was allowed two hours of preparation time with my attorney. I was also emailed two short videos to watch the day before deposition. In this preparation time I was given very specific instructions and I was told unless you are 100% sure of the answer, you are to answer "I do not recall". You're not allowed any notes that you can refer back to or paper to write on. It's not like your studying a chapter for a test, or a manual to help prepare you for the questions that lie ahead. All answers come from your memory and you may not have seen some of this paperwork for months or years. I did know most of the figures that Attorney B (my partners attorney) was asking; I just did not know the exact amounts.

In my case I had thousands of papers to refer back to with different figures that were on daily, monthly and yearly basis. I had never thought of anything I had done with the business in hours, except marketing and I had kept a log. This is where keeping a time card for the different tasks I had worked on would have come in handy.

The videos I watched, gave the same advice, do not guess or elaborate on your answer. Stick to the shortest answer you can unless it helps your case. If you are unsure of anything, even how the question is worded, the answer is "I do not recall". The wording of a question is extremely important and can change in an instant. Nothing prepared me for the chaos that I was thrown into.

The videos I watched everyone seemed pleasant and respectful to each other, very unlike mine. What you can't read in this deposition is the emotions, the volume, the expressions and the body language that was presented in that room. There were many times when it was to the point of shouting. The tension was so thick you could have cut it with a knife. My business partner was also present which was stressful for me. I had tried to not be around my partner as much as possible prior to this day.

The …..'s that you will see throughout this deposition is the conversation that was going on that the court recorder could not keep up with. She did an awesome job for the constant bantering and talking over each other going on back and forth between the attorneys. You will see a lot of •••• •••• throughout this deposition as well as the recorder stopping the deposition because of the exchanges. If I were to guess there is probably an hours' worth of communication that was not caught by the recorder. With both attorneys talking over each other, it became very difficult to keep track of what was being said during those exchanges. I always worried that Attorney 2 had thrown in a question that I did not catch.

I was told and the videos stated you have the right to a fair question. Nothing was said what to do if you felt you did not get one other than, "could you rephrase that question". The horrible questions I was given, that included lead-ins, and answers already given within them, I did not know how to address. I had no practice addressing these types of questions with the "don't you agree" as the lead off. I could honestly say I did not agree very often with attorney 2. I was not told how to address questions with more than one question in them. Nor had I been given practice or advice when someone continually asks the same question.

My attorney (1) did say to pay attention to him, watch him in case he wanted to object. Give him time to do his job, which was why he was there. He had stressed that may times, including during breaks. Because there was so much conversation going on between the attorneys, I found myself at times automatically looking at my attorney to object. My partners attorney kept telling me don't look at my attorney, but that was what I was instructed to do.

I was told my partners attorney would try to make me angry because you make more mistakes when you're angry. Attorney 2 did, many times from his condescending remarks and it's hard to come up with answers other than the answers you would like to give. Some of the answers

I would have liked to have given would not have looked good in court and I was clearly instructed not to give them. You do not want to answer in any way that will "reflect poorly on you". No matter what, you are not to get rude or use inappropriate answers; you are to stick to "I do not recall". I was instructed to use it if I needed a moment to clear my head and come up with the correct answer.

One of the things you can't hear from reading this is how fast the questioning would get. I was told do not let the attorney get into a rhythm. If I tried to slow things down or take a moment to think about an answer, it seemed the questions just kept coming or I would get "you have to answer".

The temperature in the room became a factor for me as well as it continued to go up throughout the day. It became unbearably hot with no relief towards the end of the day. I was told there was nothing they could do about it. Just remember to layer, and be prepared for the room to go either way.

I have removed a few of the paragraphs containing personal information, some words that gave implications and all of the names in this deposition. I do not want to disclose mine or any other person's personal information including those involved in this cases. They have their right to privacy and I want to respect that. Everyone's names have just become initials. These initials are the most common representations you will see throughout this deposition:

I am the plaintiff and my initial will be H.
My business partner's initial will be G.
My attorney is attorney #1
G's attorney is attorney #2

I have changed well known social media companies names and just made them all "marketing". Vendors, witnesses or other people we were in contact with I used an initial to represent them as we come to the questioning that involves them.

The personal information in this deposition is not important. The purpose of this book is to let you see how questions are asked and how the process works. If I would have seen something like this or was even able to have seen this deposition prior to trial, I know it would have helped me to give better answers in deposition and in court. If I had seen these questions, and how I had answered them in deposition, I could have been able to discuss them with my firm and asked how I could have answered them better. I feel we could have made my case stronger from this information.

Here are ten hints that I would like you to take away from my deposition to hopefully help you in yours. You will see some examples in my deposition that I bring out and state what I wish I would have done better.

1. Listen to your attorney, your attorney should have given you advice on how to handle certain ques-

tions. Keep in mind what your attorney has said when addressing difficult questions.
2. Stay focused; if you start to lose focus ask for a quick break. Take this moment to clear your head so you're ready to address the questions being asked. If you let your mind wander you will miss the true intent of the question being asked.
3. Make sure you understand the question, if you do not ask for clarification. If you are not sure you are getting a fair question ask for the question to be rephrased.
4. Stay with the same answer if you feel that is the right thing to do. It becomes very uncomfortable when you're asked the same question over and over.
5. Listen for changes in the wording of a question. Just changing two words can make such a huge difference in the meaning of a question.
6. If you are not 100% sure of an answer then the answer becomes "I do not recall". Make sure you stay with that answer no matter how uncomfortable it becomes. Your attorney should be there to support you and will guide you if they feel you should be addressing the question differently.
7. If you feel you are not getting a fair question or if there are two questions within your question ask for the question to be rephrased. Let the attorney asking you the questions know you feel there are two

separate questions and you would like to be asked one at a time.
8. Do not forget to layer in preparation for your deposition. This seems so simple, but it can become an issue with the temperature fluctuation in the room. You will not regret this.
9. After you read your deposition, highlight the questions you want to go over with your attorney. Be very clear how you should have addressed them in deposition before going into court. See if the questions are leading up to a pattern. In my case if was how I spent my off time to make it look like I could never have spent the amount of time I had on my business.
10. High light the answers you gave that you were not happy with discuss how you could have answered the question better. Re-read your answers prior to going into court.

This was typed by the court recorder and some of the gaps could not be removed. I have inserted *** for certain information that should not be disclosed, personal information or names. This will be the only thing that I have inserted or changed, with in the court recorders information. Otherwise the court recorder has documented everything else. My responses to what was going on during the deposition or how I felt about a question and how I feel I should have responded will be typed in blue. These are the area's that I feel were most important, affected court or were just appalling to me. Good luck reading this at times it gets to be too much, but it's all real. This is my crazy deposition:

IN THE SUPERIOR COURT OF THE STATE OF
CALIFORNIA IN AND FOR THE COUNTY OF PLACER

H, an individual;
"MY BUSINESS", a California general partnership,
               Plaintiffs,
vs.   No. SCV0037147

G, an individual; and DOES 1 through 100, inclusive,
               Defendants.
_____/

DEPOSITION OF H
Thursday, January 5, 2017

Reported by:
M.C.R.
CSR No. ****
Job. No. *****LR

B Kuffel

APPEARANCES

For the Plaintiffs:
  MY Attorneys Firm, address and email went here.
For the Defendants:
  G's Attorneys Firm, address and email went here.

  G

---oOo---

INDEX OF EXAMINATIONS

PAGE
5

  Examination by Attorney 2

---oOo---

INDEX OF EXHIBITS
Deposition of H
Thursday, January 5, 2017

DEPOSITION

EXHIBIT	PAGE	DESCRIPTION
1	238	Email dated February 27, 2015 re Solution??
2	240	Email dated March 3, 2015 re Meeting???

3	247	Two emails dated March 3, 2015 re Mediator
4	252	Email dated April 6, 2015 re Proposal??
5	254	Email dated March 3, 2010 re Our business
6	256	Two emails dated March 4, 2010 and March 5, 2010 re Starting a business, two pages
7	262	Three emails dated March 4, March 5 and March 8, 2010 re Starting a business, three pages
8	267	Partnership Agreement, five pages

INDEX OF RECORD MARKED

Page	Line
18	15-16
138	16-24

—oOo—

BE IT REMEMBERED that, pursuant to Notice of Taking Deposition, and on Thursday, the 5th day of January, 2017 commencing at the hour of 9:00 a.m. thereof, at the Law Offices of Attorney 2, California, before me, M. C. R, a Certified Shorthand Reporter in and for the State of California, there personally appeared H, called as a Plaintiff herein, who, having been by me duly sworn, was thereupon examined and interrogated as hereinafter set forth.

—oOo—

EXAMINATION BY ATTORNEY 2

Q. Could you state and spell your name, please.

A. B*****, B-*-*-*-*-*, *, H-*-*-*-*-*-*

Q. Ms., my name is Attorney 2, and I represent G in the lawsuit that brings us here today. You know that. And we're here to take your deposition. And so let me explain a little of the ground rules we follow today. And I'm sure your lawyer has gone through these with you, but we tend to repeat them all so you do understand them and so they're part of our record.

The court reporter sitting to your left is responsible to take down everything that we say here today, so it's important that we have some simple rules to make her job easier. It's not her responsibility to be looking at you to notice that you're nodding your head as an affirmative response, and it's not her responsibility to interpret the uh-huhs in the affirmative or a negative. So you have to answer questions audibly and in words.

A. Yes, sir.

Q. If you don't understand what I say, by all means – or what I'm asking, by all means ask me, tell me, and I'll repeat or rephrase the question so that you hear it and understand it. I'm not trying to fool you or trick you. I just want to get your best testimony of things we're going to talk about.

A. Yes, sir.

Q. It all makes sense?

A. Yes.

Q. Okay. We have to avoid talking at the same time. In normal conversation, people will anticipate what someone else is going to say and speak before someone else finishes a thought. So let me get out my whole question before you answer even if you're convinced you know what I'm going to ask.

It allows you to think about it. It allows your lawyer to object if he wants. But listen to my whole question before you answer. And if you stop and hesitate and I think you're done and I start asking another question, feel free to tell me to shut up because you weren't finished with your answer, because again I want you to get your whole answer out, okay?

A. Thank you.

Q. I don't want you to guess or speculate. If you don't know an answer, you don't know an answer. But obviously we're entitled to your best knowledge of whatever that subject happens to be because there's always something in your head which isn't in mine. So whenever you can, tell me the answer to a question. I'm entitled to your best answer. I mean there's some things obviously you have no idea about, but there's some things you maybe just don't remember or you'd have to estimate to provide a response, and we're entitled to your best response, whatever that is, okay?

A. Yes, sir.

Q. All makes sense?

A. Yes.

Q. Anytime you want to stop, take a break, just let me know. Again we're just here to find out what the pertinent facts and circumstances are.

A. Okay.

Q. Why don't you start by summarizing your education for me.

A. I was in the Air Force for six years. I started there as a s. t.. I have been with "Employer" since 1989. I got my ** in 1992. So I've been in the *** *** for 33 years.

Q. Okay.
A. I graduated from the *********..
Q. With what degree?
A. An associate's.
Q. And when was that?
A. That was in 19**.
Q. And is your only job in the ******* profession with "Employer"?
A. Correct.
Q. And which "Employer" do you presently work at?
A. "Employer" ********.
Q. And how long have you worked there?
A. I have worked there since 20**.
Q. And where did you work before that?
A. R. C.. I started there in 19** and left there and came up to ******** in 2000.
Q. So you were in R. C. for 1* years and in ******** for 1*, 1*?
A. Correct.
Q. What were your responsibilities in R.C.?
A. I started with R.C. as a s. t.. After I got my **, I became the *** *** in the ****** *** on the evening shift. I was on the evenings for 22 years. So I was the *** *** until approximately 201*, in which I moved to the day shift. And I just work as a ** now.
Q. You've gotten a little ahead of me –
A. I'm sorry.
Q. because you're answering in ********, and I only asked what you did in R.C..
A. I'm sorry. So I was a s. t. and an **, ******.

Q. And then since you've worked in ********, what have your jobs been?
A. I was the ****** until about 201*, and then I moved to the day shift.
Q. All working as an ******* –
A. I was an ********* –
Q. Wait.
A. Sorry.
Q. We need to avoid speaking at the same time.
A. I'm sorry.
Q. So the entire time you've worked as an ** **, different capacities but same title so to speak?
A. Correct.
Q. And what shifts do you presently work?
A. I work the 9:00 to 5:30 shift.
Q. Five days a week?
A. Five days a week, 40 hours a week.
Q. And how long has that been true?
A. Since around late 2011.
Q. Is that unusual, a 9:00 to 5:30 shift, for a ****?
A. It's rare for a ****. ******** is one of the few places that has a 9:00 to 5:30 shift I think.
Q. Does that overlap with other shifts that work days or –
A. ********, from what I understand, is one of the few places that has a lot of overlapping shifts.
Q. So there's still your typical three shifts?
A. Correct.
Q. And you just happen to overlap with two of those?
A. Correct.
Q. Is there a reason why that has been done, if you know?

A. We're the break shift, and then at three o'clock when the day shift go home, we go into a **** and cover a ***** at that time.
Q. Are you married?
A. Yes, sir.
Q. How long have you been married?
A. I've been married since ****.
Q. Do you have any children?
A. ***.
ATTORNEY 1: Objection, relevance.
Q. (By ATTORNEY 2) And how old are your children?
A. ** and **. I'm sorry – yeah, ** and **.
Q. What are the hobbies, if that's the right word, or primary ways you spend your non-working time?
ATTORNEY 1: That's kind of ambiguous. What do you mean by non-working? Objection. THE WITNESS: Could you clarify the question, sir, please.
Q. (By ATTORNEY 2) Sure. I'm just looking at what hobbies you have or what you otherwise do, family travel or otherwise, in your time you're away from "Employer".
ATTORNEY 1: Objection. That's compound.

> ATTORNEY 2: He can object all he wants. You still have to answer my question.

ATTORNEY 1: You can go ahead and answer.
THE WITNESS: I mainly just support my kids. They're extremely involved. So whenever they have a **** event or a *** event and **** or ****, then we usually are doing that.
Q. (By ATTORNEY 2) Your 9:00 to 5:30, that's a Monday through Friday?
A. Correct.

Q. How long have you known G?
A. I'm not sure the exact date of when I –
Q. Best estimate.
A. Maybe 2002 approximately. I'm not for sure the exact date.
Q. Within a year or two? That's probably –
A. Somewhere in there.
Q. Have you ever worked together?
A. Yes.
Q. In what capacities?
A. We were in a ***** a couple of times together.
Q. So in the plus or minus 1*, 1* years you've known G, you've only worked together on a couple of occasions?
A. In a ****. We have crossed shifts before. But working together, only a few times.
Q. So if I understand what you're telling me, you'd be working at the same time –
A. But not necessarily –
Q. – but not in the same ****?
A. Correct.
Q. When you say a ****, you're talking about an ****?
A. An ****, correct.
Q. So you've only worked together in an ****** a handful of times?
A. Correct.
Q. How frequently have you worked the same shift?
ATTORNEY 1: Objection, relevance.
THE WITNESS: Same shift, not very often.
Q. (By ATTORNEY 2) Is that once a year, once a month? What does not very often mean?
A. I don't recall.

Q. To your recollection, where did the idea of starting the "My Business" business come from? ATTORNEY 1: Objection. You're assuming facts not yet in evidence. Could you please start where she has the basis for this discussion?

Q. (By ATTORNEY 2) You can answer the question, please.
ATTORNEY 1: Could you clarify –
ATTORNEY 2: No, I'm not going to answer.
ATTORNEY 1: Well, I'm asking you -
ATTORNEY 2: I understand you are. Make your objection and we'll proceed.
ATTORNEY 1: Did you understand the objection?
ATTORNEY 2: It doesn't M.er whether you understand the objection.

Q. Do you understand the question?

A. I defer to my counsel whether or not –
ATTORNEY 1: Go ahead and answer his question.
THE WITNESS: Okay. We both came up with the idea of "My Business".

Q. (By ATTORNEY 2) What does that mean?

A. Could you please clarify the question.

Q. Sure. You say, we both came up with the idea. What idea did you come up with that evolved into "My Business"?
ATTORNEY 1: Objection. What do you mean by idea? Could you clarify? This is vague and ambiguous, your question.

Q. (By ATTORNEY 2) Ms., objections are made for the record. He can object all he wants. I am never going to respond to his objections

If you don't understand my question, you need to tell me, because I'm assuming you understand my question if you answer it. So I'm not going to pay any attention to his objections, with the exceptions there may be some things that I agree with him. But generally just because he doesn't like my question, you still have to answer.

ATTORNEY 1: And I would like you to defer to me.

THE WITNESS: I'm going to defer to my counsel.

ATTORNEY 2: You don't get to defer to him. If you do, we're going to go seek a court order right away. There's no one here that rules on objections. All objections are reserved to the time of trial. So objections are part of the record. If I want to use this transcript later, a court will rule at that time on the objection. It is as if you are instructed to answer every question anyway.

Q. So all I'm asking you at the present time is, what was your thought process? Because you told me you had some input in coming up with the concept of "My Business". So where in your mind did this concept come from?
A. So I'm deferring to my counsel.
Q. He hasn't said anything. You have to answer the question.
ATTORNEY 1: You're being argumentative and harassing of my client. I'm objecting to that. First, H and
Attorney 2 – I want to be clear – you do defer to me when I tell you not to answer a question such as a privilege of attorney/client or something of that nature. Please defer to me.
THE WITNESS: Yes, sir.
ATTORNEY 1: And please listen to my objections. And I will try to tell you when you can answer and I'm just

preserving a question, and when not to answer. I hope that will help facilitate a smoother process,

Attorney 2. Could you ask the question again?

Q. (By ATTORNEY 2) Do you understand what I asked you?

A. Could you please repeat the question?

Q. Sure. When is the first time you had the idea of running a business, any kind of business?

A. I would like to defer to my counsel.

Q. You don't get to defer to your counsel. You are required to answer my question. ATTORNEY 1: Objection, relevance of any business. We're here about a specific business.

ATTORNEY 2: No, we're not.

ATTORNEY 1: We are. We're here to talk about "My Business", sir.

ATTORNEY 2: No, we're not. I'm entitled to ask whatever I want.

ATTORNEY 1: Objection stands.

Go ahead and answer his question.

THE WITNESS: I have had several thoughts of several different businesses throughout my career.

Q. (By ATTORNEY 2) Okay. What type of businesses?

ATTORNEY 1: Objection, calls for a narrative.

ATTORNEY 2: You still have to answer.

THE WITNESS: I defer to my counsel.

ATTORNEY 2: You still have to answer. If he instructs you not to answer, we'll deal with it. ATTORNEY 1: Will you stop harassing -

ATTORNEY 2: Even if he objects, you still have to answer.

ATTORNEY 1: Could we stop raising your voice with my client.
ATTORNEY 2: I am not raising my voice.
ATTORNEY 1: You are raising your voice.
ATTORNEY 2: I am just —
ATTORNEY 1: Let the record reflect you are raising your voice and you are talking over me, and I wasn't done, Attorney 2. I'm trying to show you courtesy here. You show me courtesy. When my sentence is done, I will pause, okay. So please again stop raising your voice to my client. This is harassing, sir. Thank you.
ATTORNEY 2: I have not raised my voice one time yet. I am siGly asking questions, and you can try and harass me all you want. It will not succeed. I am just going to continue asking questions of your client. If you instruct her not to answer, that's fine. If he does not instruct you not to answer, you still have to answer my question.
ATTORNEY 1: Okay.

*** As you can see starting off, with both attorneys going back and forth at times things became overwhelming. Watching and listening to them talk I would forget the content of the question, and I was afraid I would answer incorrectly.

Q. (By ATTORNEY 2) What businesses did you ever think of opening yourself?
A. I've opened one business in the past which was a printing — a small scale printing business. I had conteGlated going back to school in order to start a different business at one

time. But at this time, I can't recall all thoughts on starting businesses.

Q. That's fine. Have you ever thought –
ATTORNEY 1: I object and move to strike that last line of questioning.
Please mark the transcript. Thank you.

Q. (By ATTORNEY 2) Have you ever thought of operating a business which had anything to do with nursing?

A. I do not recall.
ATTORNEY 1: Objection, as to -
ATTORNEY 2: The question is answered.
ATTORNEY 1: Okay. Please wait for me. Give me a second.
THE WITNESS: I'm sorry.
ATTORNEY 1: That's fine.

Q. (By ATTORNEY 2) When is the first time you had a conversation with G about running a business together?
ATTORNEY 1: Objection, hearsay.
Go ahead and answer.
THE WITNESS: It would have been approximately the last week of March 20**.

Q. (By ATTORNEY 2) And as best you can recall, could you describe that conversation to me?

A. We were –
ATTORNEY 1: Objection, calls for a narrative.
Go ahead and answer.
THE WITNESS: We were – that particular evening, we were – I was leaving; she was coming in. It was kind of a bad night, and I said, yeah, if there was other – I wish that I had other opportunities that I could have instead of just

working here. And we had a conversation around that. The rest of it, I don't really recall.

*** I wish I had taken a moment to clear my thoughts, and answered the question the way I thought it over in my head. I was trying to be careful in answering the questions.

Q. (By ATTORNEY 2) Did you approach G and say, would you like to run a business with me?
ATTORNEY 1: Objection, relevance.
Go ahead and answer.
THE WITNESS: No.
Q. (By ATTORNEY 2) Did G approach you and say, I have an idea that I'd like to talk to you about running a business together?
A. Yes.
Q. And that's this conversation in March of 20**?
ATTORNEY 1: You're mischaracterizing her statement. Are you asking, was that the totality? It's vague and ambiguous also. But is that the totality of the conversation, or was that what was entailed in that conversation? Could you please clarify your question.
ATTORNEY 2: You need to answer my questions and not his.
ATTORNEY 1: It was vague and ambiguous

*** Sorry for the large gaps. I am unable to change what the court reporter typed, and I cannot eliminate these large gaps. There will be a few throughout this book.

B Kuffel

> Could you please clarify -
> ATTORNEY 2: No. I will not repeat my questions.
> ATTORNEY 1: Did you understand -
> ATTORNEY 2: Answer the question.
> ATTORNEY 1: No, you don't order my client to answer questions,
> Attorney 2. I'm asking her, did you understand the question? If you understood the question, you can answer. If you would like more clarification -
> THE WITNESS: I would like more clarification of that particular question.

Q. (By ATTORNEY 2) You've said that G came to you and raised the subject of possibly doing some business together, correct? Is that correct?

A. Yes.

Q. Was that the conversation you earlier alluded to that happened in March of 20**?

> ATTORNEY 1: Same objection. It's unclear whether or not you're asking whether that was the totality of the conversation or if that was what was stated as part of the conversation. Could you please clarify.
> ATTORNEY 2: Please answer my question.
> ATTORNEY 1: Do you understand –
> ATTORNEY 2: He's trying to ask me to ask you a totally different question than I want to ask you. That's why I'm going to totally ignore him. You get to answer my questions, not his. If you don't understand what I ask, you need to tell me that. Because he wants me to ask you a different question, and I'm not going to, okay? Do you understand that? I'm asking questions. He's not. ATTORNEY 1:

Would you like clarification of Attorney 2 on the issues I raised?

THE WITNESS: Could you please clarify the question.

ATTORNEY 2: Could you repeat the last question, please.

(Whereupon the record "Question: You've said that G came to you and raised the subject of possibly doing some business together, correct? Is that correct? Answer: Yes. Question: Was that the conversation you earlier alluded to that happened in March of 20**" was read back as requested.)

ATTORNEY 1: Same objection stands. I believe the question is vague and ambiguous. And my client would need clarification as to what specifically you mean.

ATTORNEY 2: You still have to answer. He hasn't instructed you not to answer. ATTORNEY 1: Do you need further clarification from Attorney 2? If you would like further clarification, you can request further clarification.

THE WITNESS: I would prefer clarification on how you're wording the question, yes.

Q. (By ATTORNEY 2) All I'm asking is when it took place. That's all I'm asking.

ATTORNEY 1: Go ahead.

THE WITNESS: The conversation took place in March of 2010.

Q. (By ATTORNEY 2) So the answer to my question after all that was, yes, it took place in – because all I asked was, did it take place in March of 2010?

That's all I asked.

ATTORNEY 1: Thank you for clarifying.

THE WITNESS: The conversation took -

ATTORNEY 2: It took 20 minutes from your lawyer to answer yes, correct?

Q. The answer is yes? It took place in March of 2010?
A. Correct.
ATTORNEY 1: Asked and answered, objection.
Go ahead.
Q. (By ATTORNEY 2) What else was discussed in that conversation?
ATTORNEY 1: Objection. You're assuming facts that there was additional topics and issues discussed, and she hasn't said that there is such information.
Q. (By ATTORNEY 2) What else was discussed in that conversation?
A. I defer to my attorney.
Q. What else was discussed in that conversation?
ATTORNEY 1: If you understood the question, you can go ahead and answer. And objecting on grounds of hearsay.
You can go ahead and answer if you like.
THE WITNESS: Based on the previous conversation that we had, we both had agreed to start a business.
Q. (By ATTORNEY 2) So this was not your first conversation about a business with G, it sounds like?
A. The conversation that we had the following day in March of 2015, we had decided based on the previous evening's conversation to start a business.
Q. Okay. You just said March of 2015. I'm assuming you mean March of 2010.
A. I'm sorry, 2010.
Q. So you just described two conversations, one on a previous evening. I want to talk about the very, very first conversation in which you and she ever discussed having a possible business together. What do you recall being discussed in

that conversation? In other words, what I'm asking you is tell me everything you remember you saying and everything you remember G saying.

ATTORNEY 1: Objection. Again she hasn't indicated that beyond what she's already stated that she recalls anything else being said. So maybe you should ask her that question before asking her this question,

Attorney 2. That might be helpful.

ATTORNEY 2: Please answer my question.

THE WITNESS: I defer to my attorney.

ATTORNEY 2: Again he's not instructing you not to answer. He's just making an objection. You still have to answer that question.

ATTORNEY 1: You can go ahead and answer that, yeah.

THE WITNESS: Based on our conversation, we decided to start a business.

Q. (By ATTORNEY 2) "Based on our conversation." I'm asking about the conversation.

So the very first conversation which you had, which it sounds like was one evening -

ATTORNEY 1: Objection, asked and answered.

Q. (By ATTORNEY 2) – I want to know what was said in that conversation. ATTORNEY 1: Objection, asked and answered.

THE WITNESS: I defer to my attorney.

ATTORNEY 1: It's been asked and answered. Move on, Attorney 2.

ATTORNEY 2: She still hasn't told me one word of -

ATTORNEY 1: Maybe ask another question.

THE WITNESS: I do not recall everything that was said in that conversation.

Q. (By ATTORNEY 2) Tell me anything that you recall that was said. ATTORNEY 1: She just said she doesn't recall. She's already answered your question, Attorney 2. Can you ask another question.

Q. (By ATTORNEY 2) Tell me everything that you recall that was said in that conversation. ATTORNEY 1: Objection, asked and answered.

Q. (By ATTORNEY 2) If your answer is, I don't recall anything that was said, tell me that. ATTORNEY 1: Objection. You're mischaracterizing what she just said. She has answered your question, Attorney 2. So maybe you should ask another related question. It might be helpful if you were to do that. We could move on.
ATTORNEY 2: You still need to answer my question.
ATTORNEY 1: My objection stands.
If you don't recall, you don't recall.
Whatever. She's answered your question.
THE WITNESS: I don't recall everything that was stated in that conversation.
ATTORNEY 2: Thank you.

Q. "I don't recall everything that was stated." That infers you recall some things that were stated. What I'm asking you is to tell me whatever it is you do recall.

A. I was talking about what my dream was, was to start a children's learning program.

Q. And that's the conversation the night before.
And then the next day, you started talking about maybe a nursing business; is that correct?
ATTORNEY 1: Objection. Ambiguous as to when the night before is. The night before what? The first conversation? The second conversation? Could you please clarify, sir.

ATTORNEY 2: Go ahead.

THE WITNESS: I defer to my attorney?

ATTORNEY 1: Would you like clarification from Attorney 2? If you understood his question, you can answer it. But if you think the question is ambiguous or you would like further explanation from him, then by all means ask him. But if you understood his question, you feel, then you can answer it.

THE WITNESS: Could we please repeat the question. (Whereupon the last question "And that's the conversation the night before. And then the next day, you started talking about maybe a **** business; is that correct" was read back as requested.)

THE WITNESS: We had discussed opening up a business offering **s.

Q. (By ATTORNEY 2) And **s means c***** education?

A. Correct.

Q. You said "we had discussed." In this first conversation or in this second one? Which time?

A. We discussed the starting of a business together in the second conversation.

Q. What do you recall discussing in that second conversation other than what you've just said?

A. There was very little discussed in that second conversation other than let's start a business.

Q. When is the next time that you and G had a conversation about the business which became "My Business"?

ATTORNEY 1: Objection, calls for hearsay testimony. You can answer.

THE WITNESS: I don't recall.

Q. (By ATTORNEY 2) Days later? Weeks later? Months later?

ATTORNEY 1: Asked and answered. She says she doesn't recall.

THE WITNESS: I don't recall the exact days. There were conversations in the next couple of days following.

Q. (By ATTORNEY 2) How many conversations?

A. I don't recall.

Q. One, two, ten? Give me your best estimate.

A. My best estimate would be one to two.

Q. And one to two conversations over a few days?

A. Correct.

Q. What do you recall, if anything, being said in those conversations?

A. The processes of starting a business.

Q. Did you discuss the processes of starting a business before you discussed the scope of what the business would be?

ATTORNEY 1: Objection, vague and ambiguous as to what scope means. If you could please clarify what you're asking.

THE WITNESS: Could I please have you clarify that question.

Q. (By ATTORNEY 2) Okay. You said you discussed CEs.

What did you discuss about **s?

A. Having them as an online ******.

Q. So at some point you had the concept of you would have a business that offered online c*** *****?

A. Correct.

Q. And then you said earlier you discussed the process of forming a business. What I was asking is, did you discuss the process of forming a business before you discussed the concept of the business of which you just said was offering online education?

ATTORNEY 1: Objection. I still think it's a vague and ambiguous question. Could you please clarify that for her. You can answer if you understood it, but I still think it's a very vague and ambiguous question. THE WITNESS: Could you please clarify the question.

Q. (By ATTORNEY 2) Okay. If I understand what you're telling me, you've described two very different subject M.ers: The substance of a business which you said was offering continuing education classes, and you also discussed the process of starting a business, right?

A. Correct.

Q. Which did you discuss first?

ATTORNEY 1: Objection. I still think it's vague as to what you mean by substance of business. What do you mean by that? Could you clarify that for her.

THE WITNESS: Could you clarify, please, sir.

Q. (By ATTORNEY 2) No. You said it. Your words, not mine. You just said the substance of the business was offering continuing education online. Those were your words; is that correct?

A. Yes, sir.

Q. That's what I mean.

ATTORNEY 1: Objection, mischaracterizing what her testimony is. That's not what she said.

ATTORNEY 2: You just said – she just said yes in response to it. That's what I'm calling the substance because those were your words. I'm coGaring the -

THE WITNESS: I would like to retract my answer -

ATTORNEY 2: That's fine.

THE WITNESS: – and have you please rephrase that question.

Q. (By ATTORNEY 2) Do you agree that what you meant as the substance of the business was some business by which you would offer c**** ***** online?

A. I don't recall what I previously said at this moment. So could you please rephrase the question.

Q. What did you understand was going to be the substance of the business that you could potentially run with G?

ATTORNEY 1: Objection as to what you mean by – vague and ambiguous. Vague as to what you mean by substance in your question. Could you please -

THE WITNESS: Could you please clarify. What do you mean by substance?

Q. (By ATTORNEY 2) You used the word, not me.

What was the business to be?

A. Offering *.****.

Q. So that's the substance of the business, right? Offering *.*.?

A. Yes.

Q. Okay. Same words you've used eight times now.

So I'm using that as one series of issues. The substance of the business was offering *.*.Es. The process, your words again, were starting the business. Do you understand the difference between substance and process?

ATTORNEY 1: Objection, compound.

Q. (By ATTORNEY 2) It's a yes or no question.

Do you understand the difference?

*** I was becoming very frustrated with the questions, and was trying to think of a way to pause to collect my thoughts before moving forward. It seemed to me I was answering the same questions over and over. I knew this was leading to something, but I was not sure what.

A. I defer to my attorney.

***My attorney told me I could defer to him, and he would help me when he could.

Q. Do you understand –
ATTORNEY 1: You can answer if you understand the difference. THE WITNESS: I understand the difference. ATTORNEY 1: Objection.

Q. (By ATTORNEY 2) What I'm asking is, which did you discuss first, substance or process?

***I was wondering where attorney 2 was going with this.

A. Process.
Q. Tell me what you discussed about the process of starting a business.
A. Seeking out a business license, contacting the BRN with an application, putting together a course to be offered to the ***.
Q. Anything else that you remember?
A. No.
Q. What did you discuss about substance?

A. We decided to create a **** course together to send to the *** to have our application approved.

Q. And *** is B *** ****?

A. *** of **** *****.

Q. Thank you. Prior to 2010, how did you track your own c*** *****?

ATTORNEY 1: Objection, relevance.

Again answer if you understood.

THE WITNESS: You sought out a company that offered ****, and you chose a course that was as close to relevance of your ****** as possible.

Q. (By ATTORNEY 2) I didn't ask how you took the course. How did you track your own *****, is what I'm asking?

A. They usually gave you a certificate, and you put it in your own records.

Q. How did you find classes that were available to let you – that you wanted to take?

ATTORNEY 1: Objection as to relevance.

Again what does this have to do with the price of tea in China?

THE WITNESS: I defer to my attorney.

ATTORNEY 1: It calls for a narrative. If you can answer the question, go ahead. I still don't think it's relevant, but if you can -otherwise, I'm going to move to strike it from the record. Go ahead.

THE WITNESS: Either by fliers in the mail, online messages sent or looking for courses through the Internet.

Q. (By ATTORNEY 2) When you and G first came up with the idea of starting a business, where did the name come from?

A. I chose the name.

Q. You're absolutely certain about that?
A. One hundred percent positive.
ATTORNEY 1: Asked and answered.
Q. (By ATTORNEY 2) Where did the name come from?
A. I was sitting at home thinking about it, and I came to that name.
Q. And how did you convey your thoughts to G?
A. In our encounter on the passing on the evening shift, I told her, what did she think about "My Business".
Q. When you first came up with the concept of going into business together, what was the primary goal in your mind of forming a business?
ATTORNEY 1: Objection, vague and ambiguous as to primary goal. Could you please explain that for Ms. .
THE WITNESS: Could you please clarify the question.
Q. (By ATTORNEY 2) Do you understand what the word "primary" means?
A. Yes, sir.
Q. Do you understand what the word "goal" means?
A. Yes, sir.
Q. Then what was the primary goal of forming a business?
ATTORNEY 1: Objection, vague and ambiguous. While she understands what the words are, she doesn't necessarily understand what you mean by the word. So if you could please provide your definition, Attorney 2, that would be very helpful.
Q. (By ATTORNEY 2) Ms., let me explain to you a little bit about depositions and his reason for being here today. There's now a limit on the time that we're allowed to spend in depositions, okay? And I have been doing this for ** years. I've taken hundreds of thousands – thousands of

depositions. I have taught classes in how to take depositions. I sit through depositions where not a word is spoken by the other lawyer. When his boss takes my client's deposition, I don't expect I'm going to say a word for the whole time the deposition takes. But there's a time limit that I'm allowed to take depositions, and I'm only allowed to ask you questions for seven hours. And it is clear that Attorney 1's thinking is that if he could talk for four of those seven hours, that's four hours less that I get to ask you questions. So at the end of the day today when we don't finish this deposition because of his actions, I fully intend to take it to the court and ask to continue your deposition until we're done. So we can sit here as long as it takes. I'm going to continue to ask very simple yes or no questions. And if he wants to object, he has the right to object, and I don't get to tell him not to. But no one gets to tell you not to answer the questions. If he instructs you not to answer, that's fine. That's his prerogative, and I'm not going to interfere with that.

But other than that, just because he calls every one of my questions vague, you still have to answer. He can talk to me all day long. It won't break my train of thought. It won't get me to lose my focus. I'm not new at this. I'm just going to keep asking you questions as many times as I need to to get you to answer them. So the question in front of you right now is, when you and G came up with the idea of starting a business together, I'm asking you what your thought process was and what in your mind was the primary goal of running or forming or operating this business. ATTORNEY 1: Objection.

Q. (By ATTORNEY 2) That is the question in front of you.

ATTORNEY 1: Objection, vague and ambiguous as to primary goal. If you understand – if you understand his question, you can answer. If it is – if my objection – excuse me. If you believe it's vague and ambiguous and would like additional clarification, by all means ask him for that. And he doesn't have to give it to you, but it will be on the record that you didn't understand the question.

So would you like additional clarification, or do you feel that you can answer the question?

THE WITNESS: I feel there's more than one component to that question.

Q. (By ATTORNEY 2) Tell me all of them.

ATTORNEY 1: Objection, compound. Oh, gosh. THE WITNESS: So I feel the primary goal of this business was to create courses to be offered in order to make money for the company.

Q. (By ATTORNEY 2) Were there other goals?

ATTORNEY 1: Objection, vague.

*** The bantering back and forth became frustrating, and hard to sit through in this room.

THE WITNESS: I'm not sure what that question -what you're asking. ATTORNEY 1: Goals for who?

ATTORNEY 2: That's fine.

Q. You just told me that that was your primary goal. Did you have other goals in mind?

ATTORNEY 1: Okay.

THE WITNESS: The goals that we were – of this company was to create courses and make money and to move the company into a better position to make money as best we could.

> *** In my mind I was thinking, "be careful with your answer, only answer the question". I wanted to stop talking because I felt I was saying too much.

Q. (By ATTORNEY 2) Okay. The idea of going into partnership together, in fact wasn't that G's idea?
A. We both decided to create this business.

> *** I should have just answered no.

Q. That's not what I'm asking you.
   The idea of becoming partners in this business, wasn't it G's idea?
   ATTORNEY 1: Objection, vague and ambiguous. What do you mean by becoming partners?
   THE WITNESS: We both decided to start this business.
Q. (By ATTORNEY 2) Did G come to you and say, "I have a business in mind, I'd like you to be my partner"? Did that ever happen?
A. G approached me –
   ATTORNEY 1: Objection, calls for hearsay testimony. If you recall and understand his – if you recall what was said and understand his question, you can answer.
   THE WITNESS: When G came in, we decided to start the business together.
Q. (By ATTORNEY 2) That's not what I'm asking. Let me make this real simple, true or false. G came to you and said, "I'd like you to be my partner in a business"?
   ATTORNEY 1: Objection, hearsay –
Q. (By ATTORNEY 2) True or false?
   ATTORNEY 1: – and vague and ambiguous.

But if you understand, you can answer.

THE WITNESS: G came to me and stated, let's start a business.

Q. (By ATTORNEY 2) Do you recall telling her you were thrilled that she had asked you to be her partner?

A. I do not recall that.

Q. When you say, I do not recall that, is that saying it didn't happen or you just don't remember whether it happened or not?

A. I do not recall that.

Q. When you decided to start this particular business, at the time of the formation – not years later – but at the time of formation, did you perceive that you would be serving other than the "Employer" nurses with whom you worked?

ATTORNEY 1: Objection, vague. What do you mean by serving?

THE WITNESS: I defer to my attorney.

ATTORNEY 1: Did you understand what he meant by serving "Employer"?

I don't understand what you mean by it.

But if you do, you can answer by all means.

THE WITNESS: Our goal was to be a company that offered *** to **** nationwide.

Q. (By ATTORNEY 2) Was that your initial goal before forming the business?

A. Our initial goal was to offer *Es on the
Internet to ***** nationwide.

Q. So when you first started the business, did you expect that you would be providing that service to nurses other than those with whom you worked at "Employer"?

A. Yes.

Q. Did you ever prepare a business plan, you, personally? A business plan for "My Business"?
A. Yes. In my mind I had a business plan.
Q. So you had ideas in your head.
Did that business plan ever get reduced to writing?
A. Not writing.
Q. What does it mean when you say not writing?
It just stayed in your head?
A. We had verbal conversations about how we wanted to grow our business.
Q. Do you understand what a business plan is?
A. Yes, sir.
Q. What do you understand a business plan to be?
A. A way to help your business grow and how you plan to get there.
Q. Did G ever show you a business plan that she had prepared?
A. I do not recall her showing me a business plan.
Q. Did you ever work on one together?
A. No.
Q. How did you – did you make some effort to determine what it would cost to start a business?
A. Yes.
Q. Was that in writing?
A. No.
Q. Did you make any effort to determine what it would cost to operate a business?
ATTORNEY 1: Objection, vague and ambiguous as to what you mean by operate.
ATTORNEY 2: You still get to answer.
ATTORNEY 1: If you understand it, you can answer it. If you would like clarification. I think it is vague as to

My Crazy Deposition

what is meant by operating and in what capacity, what sense? Overhead? What are we talking about? Clarification would be helpful. The business expenses? What are we talking about, Attorney 2?

THE WITNESS: Could you please clarify that question.

> ***I was trying to follow my attorneys lead, even if I did not know where it was going at times. I thought I may have missed something in a trick question.

ATTORNEY 2: Could you read the question back.
(Whereupon the last question "Did you make any effort to determine what it would cost to operate a business" was read back as requested.)

Q. (By ATTORNEY 2) Let me just be more specific. Did you personally make an effort to determine what it would cost to operate "My Business"?

ATTORNEY 1: Objection, vague as to determine. Go ahead and answer. THE WITNESS: Those costs were discovered as we moved forward with the business.

Q. (By ATTORNEY 2) Okay. But what I'm asking is, before you start business, when you're in the planning stage of the business, did you make an effort to estimate what it would cost to run that business?

A. That was hard to plan out without contacting companies to find out what their expenses were. And as we were building the business, we contacted companies to find out those expenses.

Q. So it sounds like you're telling me the answer is no as to the formation stage, right?

ATTORNEY 1: Objection. You're mischaracterizing -

THE WITNESS: I'm not saying no.
ATTORNEY 1: – what she said.
But I mean you can answer.
THE WITNESS: I did not say no to that question. It was difficult to have clear ideas of costs without contacting businesses to know what those costs were.

Q. (By ATTORNEY 2) So is the answer you tried to do it, but you were unsuccessful?
A. No, sir, I didn't say that.
Q. Then I'm trying to understand what you are telling me. What I'm looking to do is, before you start the business, you're in the planning stage, I want to know all the steps you undertook to estimate what it would cost you once you started that business to run it on an ongoing basis. So you've explained it was difficult to do so. So the question seems to me, as you're saying, it was difficult so we were unable to do so?
A. I didn't say that.
ATTORNEY 1: Objection, compound. There's not a question
Q. (By ATTORNEY 2) So what were –
(Reporter interruption.)

> ***This was the first of many reporter interruptions due to the constant talking from more than one person at a time. She reminded us all, that she could only have one person talking at a time.

Q. (By ATTORNEY 2) So what were you able to do?
A. I started to contact companies to find out costs.
Q. What companies did you contact?

My Crazy Deposition

A. I was contacting different web gentlemen to find out what it would cost to build a website. We both were searching the Internet for a testing company. And trying to see what different prices were. And we estimated our costs would be after we kind of put all that together.

Q. What did you estimate your costs to be after you put all that together?

A. I do not recall.

Q. Do you have any recollection at all?

A. I do not recall.

Q. Is it more than ten thousand dollars a month?

A. I do not recall.

Q. You don't recall before you started the business whether you thought it was going to cost you more or less than ten thousand dollars?

A. I do not recall.
ATTORNEY 1: Objection, asked and answered.
Sorry.

Q. (By ATTORNEY 2) Is it more –
ATTORNEY 1: I object. Asked and answered.
(Reporter interruption.)

> ***This was the second interruption within a short time to tell them to stop the talking over each other, and you can tell from the "••••" she was having a hard time documenting what was being said.

ATTORNEY 1: And we should really just move on from the question. She's already said she doesn't recall like three or four times, so she's already said that.

Q. (By ATTORNEY 2) When you prepared these estimates, did you understand it would cost you more than a hundred thousand dollars a month to run your business?

A. Could you please clarify that question.

Q. Right. Easy. You figured out it was going to cost you something to run a month a business. If you had decided at the beginning of the business that it would cost you, for example, one million dollars per month, you presumably would never have started the business, right, because you couldn't afford a million dollars a month; is that fair?

A. Yes, sir.

Q. When you did this analysis, did you determine that it would cost more than one hundred thousand dollars a month?

> *** I realized he was putting his words in my answers, but I was not sure how to stop how he was asking these questions. I did not feel these were "fair" questions. In court I realized the words he was using, he used against me. His comments became my answers during trial. I should have said the same answer every time, and commented what he was saying was incorrect.

A. No, sir.

Q. It was going to cost less than that?

A. Yes, sir.

Q. Was it going to cost less than fifty thousand dollars a month?

A. Yes, sir.

Q. Was it going to cost less than twenty-five thousand dollars a month?

ATTORNEY 1: Objection. The question is vague as to when you say per month. Are you talking about at start-up stage? Down the road? What are you talking about? Could you –

Q. (By ATTORNEY 2) Was it less than twenty-five thousand dollars a month?

A. Yes, sir.

Q. Was it less than ten thousand dollars a month?

ATTORNEY 1: Objection. It's still vague as to what you mean by per month. When? At what point? What period of time? That's a very valid objection. At what point in time are you speaking about, Attorney 2? Down the road if it became a Fortune 500 company or a start-up? I don't know what you're talking about.

ATTORNEY 2: He wants to save three minutes to object to a yes or no question every time. You've answered the question six times. You obviously understand it. He's just trying to waste my time. It's okay.

It's his prerogative.

Q. The question again is, you've answered the same question using the expenses of a million dollars a month, five hundred thousand dollars a month, a hundred thousand, fifty thousand, twenty-five. I'm now asking you that identical question, which you've answered six times, did you determine that it would cost you less than ten thousand dollars a month?

A. Yes.

ATTORNEY 1: Same objection.

ATTORNEY 2: Thank you.

Q. Did you determine it would cost you less than five thousand dollars a month?

ATTORNEY 1: Same objection as vague and ambiguous as to what month you're talking about. And also the question calls for speculation. But go ahead and answer if you recall.

THE WITNESS: At the time of start-up, it was less than five thousand dollars a month.

ATTORNEY 2: Thank you. That's what I'm asking you.

Q. Was it less than twenty-five hundred dollars a month?
A. Yes.
Q. Was it less than two thousand dollars a month?
A. At start-up, we didn't know that at that time.
Q. So now at least I have your best recollection of it was something in the thousand to twenty-five hundred dollars to start up, right?
A. At that time we didn't know the exact costs that it would be per month.
Q. How did you decide where to seek customers?

ATTORNEY 1: Objection, vague and ambiguous as to what you mean by customers. You can answer if you understand.

THE WITNESS: We were going to be an Internet company, and we were going to seek customers from the Internet.

Q. (By ATTORNEY 2) How were you going to drive people to know that your business existed?

ATTORNEY 1: Objection. What do you mean by drive people to know it existed? Objection, vague and ambiguous.

THE WITNESS: Could you please clarify that question.

My Crazy Deposition

Q. (By ATTORNEY 2) Sure. You assumed, it sounds like, that your customers were going to find the business online, right?

A. Yes, sir.

Q. How did you think that was possible?

A. When I discovered J and was able to talk to J, who was our initial web designer, he stated he knew how to guide customers to our website.

Q. Who is J?

A. J is the original gentleman who designed and created our website. I'm blank on J's last name at the moment.

Q. Does he have a business name?

A. Yes, but at this time I can't remember the name.

Q. So just someone named J who gave you some advice about using the Internet to drive customers to your business? That's who he is?

A. J was not some guy. He was the gentleman that designed and created our website.

Q. So you did hire him, and he did do some work for you?

A. Correct, sir.

Q. And you just don't remember his name?

ATTORNEY 1: Asked and answered. THE WITNESS: I don't remember his exact last name at this moment.

Q. (By ATTORNEY 2) Was he a sole proprietor?

A. Yes.

Q. When you were in these planning stages deciding whether or not to start a business or how to start a business, did you seek any advice from third parties?

ATTORNEY 1: Objection, calls for hearsay testimony. Answer it.

THE WITNESS: No.

Q. (By ATTORNEY 2) Did you ever meet with a lawyer about starting a new business?
A. No.
Q. Did you meet with an accountant about starting a new business?
A. No.
Q. Did you meet with any form of business advisor about starting a new business?
A. No.
Q. When do you feel you actually made the decision to go ahead and start the business together?
ATTORNEY 1: Objection. I think she's already answered this. It was in her prior testimony about when they started the business and had those conversations. There were two conversations. But go ahead and answer the question. I just think this is duplicative and -
THE WITNESS: When I presented the partnership agreement with G and we actually signed the agreement.
Q. (By ATTORNEY 2) I assume you had to have made the decision prior to that; otherwise, you wouldn't have prepared the partnership agreement, right?
A. Yes.
Q. So how far in advance of preparing the partnership agreement did you feel that you had some oral understanding, yes, let's go ahead with this?
A. A few days.
Q. When do you believe that was?
A. Could you please clarify that question.
Q. Sure. What month? What year?
A. The question, I didn't understand the question prior to the date.

My Crazy Deposition

Q. I'm asking – you said you had the okay, you felt you had reached an accord to start a business together, a few days before you actually presented a partnership agreement, right?

ATTORNEY 1: Objection. I think you said that, and you asked her if that was correct, and she confirmed it. And then she just now said she was confused by the questions and would like clarification. So could you maybe back up before –

Q. (By ATTORNEY 2) Do you believe you've testified wrong? Did you make some mistakes somewhere?

Do you believe you've said something incorrect?

> ***It is a mistake to get frustrated and answer questions like this. Stop and ask the person asking you this question, "What question do you want me to answer? I have heard you ask me three questions". You're not allowed to take notes; you have to answer on the fly. Try to get one question so you are not trying to remember the other questions.

A. Not at this time.

Q. So let me ask the question again if your lawyer doesn't think you've answered it. At what point in time do you feel that you and G made the decision that you were going to go ahead and start a business together?

A. April 1st when we signed the partnership agreement.

Q. April 1st what year?

A. 2010.

Q. So I assume that you had some oral understanding that you were going to proceed before a partnership agreement was written -
ATTORNEY 1: Objection.
Q. (By ATTORNEY 2) – because you wouldn't have prepared the partnership agreement - ATTORNEY 1: Speculation, iGroper hypothetical.
ATTORNEY 2: There's no question pending, so no basis to object.
Q. You prepared a partnership agreement at some point, right?
A. Yes, sir.
Q. Is it fair to say you would not have prepared that partnership agreement unless you already had concluded that there was a partnership to document?

> *** In this objection when "legal conclusion" was brought up, I was thinking to myself "is this some kind of trick question" "Why did he object, is it to give me a chance to rethink the question?" "To warn me"? There were so many things going through my mind.

ATTORNEY 1: Objection, calls for a legal conclusion.
THE WITNESS: I defer to my attorney.
ATTORNEY 2: You still have to answer the question.
ATTORNEY 1: I think it calls for a legal conclusion, that she's not qualified. She's not an expert qualified to answer that question.
ATTORNEY 2: You still have to answer it.
ATTORNEY 1: If you don't understand the question, you can ask for clarification – or I mean you can answer the

question to the best of your knowledge, but I don't think you're qualified to answer his question because it calls for a legal conclusion that she is not qualified to make. She's a lay person, and you're asking a question that goes to the ultimate facts concerning creation of a partnership.

Q. (By ATTORNEY 2) Do you have the question in mind? He's not going to break my train of thought. He's clearly breaking yours. Do you have the question in mind anymore after his five-minute rampage? Do you know what I asked you?

> *** After these long exchanges I wanted to make sure I had the wording of the questions correct before I moved on, and make sure that a question wasn't thrown into the mix that I would be answering for.

ATTORNEY 1: I'm glad you –
THE WITNESS: Why don't you clarify the question, please.
ATTORNEY 2: Sure, sure.

Q. Why did you prepare a written partnership agreement?
A. We had discussed starting a business. And from that discussion, we then – I then prepared a partnership agreement.
Q. Why did you prepare the agreement?
A. Because we had decided to go into business.
Q. Exactly. That's the point I made before.

> *** Now I would worry did I miss any point from before and was this a lead into some trick question? I was already really stressed going into this process; now what point was made before?

So when did you come to the point where you acknowledged in your head that you had made that decision?

I assume the answer is a day or two before you prepared the agreement.

A. A day or two —

ATTORNEY 1: Do you want to testify for -

ATTORNEY 2: Thank you.

ATTORNEY 1: — her, Attorney 2?

(Reporter interruption.)

> *** The court reporter was getting frustrated. Each time she interrupted the talking, she would tell the attorneys to stop and talk one at a time. You could tell she was getting frustrated with this bantering.

THE WITNESS: I would like to clarify my answer.

Q. (By ATTORNEY 2) Go right ahead.

A. I don't recall exactly how many days prior to the — to signing the agreement when the decision was to proceed with the business.

Q. But it was a few days, whether one or two or five? It was a few days, right?

> *** This is a great example of how words were being put in my mouth. Do not fall for this.

ATTORNEY 1: Objection. You're putting words in her mouth and trying to get her to agree to them. She's already said she doesn't recall, so can we leave it at that. What's the purpose -

ATTORNEY 2: I will never accept "I don't recall" as an answer. So you make your objections, and I'll ask my questions.

> ***It is difficult to answer when he says, "'I never accept I don't recall...' as an answer". This is what you are taught to say, and he never accepts it.

Q. Please answer my questions.
ATTORNEY 1: Asked and answered. The question has been asked and answered. Let's move on.
THE WITNESS: I don't recall the exact time frame. It was – I don't recall the exact time frame.

> ***I'm still thinking to myself, "What am I supposed to answer if he will not accept 'I do not recall'"?

Q. (By ATTORNEY 2) You said a few days, right?
THE WITNESS: Could I please have a drink of water?

> ***This is when it appeared the temperature had been turned up; it started to get warm in the room. The court recorder was wearing a sleeveless shirt. That should have told me something. Even though you might be dressing for winter or summer be prepared to layer.

ATTORNEY 2: Sure. Why don't you get it. It's right here.
THE WITNESS: Thank you.
ATTORNEY 1: Sure.

Q. (By ATTORNEY 2) So you reach this understanding a few days before you signed the agreement, right?

> ***I'm trying to drink my water, and the questions have already started.

ATTORNEY 1: I'm sorry, can we go off the record while she drinks her water, just give her a minute to -
ATTORNEY 2: Do you need a break, or can we continue?
THE WITNESS: I just need a drink of water. My throat is getting extremely dry. It's kind of warm in here.
ATTORNEY 1: There's a lot of things in here.
THE WITNESS: Working in the *** ****, it's usually much colder. Okay.

> *** This was a huge mistake. I should have never said this; the temperature went way up after this.

Q. (By ATTORNEY 2) Your last words were, a few days. All I'm trying to understand is what you mean when you say a few.

> *** In this line of questioning I should have just said "I believe I have answered that question". Thinking back, I should have used this answer when he kept asking the same question.

ATTORNEY 1: Objection. You're mischaracterizing her last words. Could we look - ATTORNEY 2: No.
Q. Answer the question, please.
A. I defer to my attorney for the moment.

Q. Okay. How many days to the best of your recollection did you and G have an agreement or oral understanding before you signed the partnership agreement?
ATTORNEY 1: Asked and answered.
THE WITNESS: As far as I know –

> *** I should have just said "I have answered that question", and stuck to that answer.

ATTORNEY 1: She says she doesn't recall.
THE WITNESS: I don't recall the exact time frame, but I believe it was in a couple days.
Q. (By ATTORNEY 2) Okay. A couple is less than a week?
A. I don't know, sir.

> *** As part of my attorney's instructions I was supposed to say "I do not recall", and to never say "I don't know".

Q. Well, what do you mean? It's your words. What do you mean when you use the word, a couple?
ATTORNEY 1: Objection, asked and answered. You're asking her to speculate what she doesn't – she clearly stated she doesn't recall. This was in 2010. I don't remember what happened last year. Can you accept that she might not recall whether it was a week, a day or a month?
ATTORNEY 2: Are you finished speaking now?
ATTORNEY 1: I just want you to be reasonable with my client, Attorney 2. This is absurd.
ATTORNEY 2: Answer my question.
THE WITNESS: I don't recall the exact day.

Q. (By ATTORNEY 2) I understand that. You said a couple of days. All I'm asking is, what do you mean when you say a couple? Is a couple – is it fair for me to assume that a couple is less than seven?

A. Yes.

Q. It is less than five?

A. A couple of days could be up to five days. I don't know.

Q. Thank you. Thank you. That's fine. Did you prepare the partnership agreement?

A. Yes, sir.

Q. Did anyone help you prepare the partnership agreement?

A. No, sir.

Q. Where did you get the format that you used which became the written partnership agreement other than – I don't want you to tell me anything that you've discussed with the lawyer, but you've already told me you hadn't consulted with a lawyer. So tell me where you got that form. ATTORNEY 1: Could you just pause between questions. He's quick, and I want to be able to hear and process the question.
THE WITNESS: I'm sorry.
ATTORNEY 1: Could you ask that question again?
THE WITNESS: Could you please repeat the question.

Q. (By ATTORNEY 2) Where did you get the form you used?

A. I bought a N partnership program.

Q. So you bought online or somewhere a form of a contract? ATTORNEY 1: Objection.
THE WITNESS: No, sir. I bought a N program that comes on a disk, and you fill in those blanks.

Q. (By ATTORNEY 2) At the point in time where you're now ready to start your business – and again I'm looking at your frame of mind, your thought processes at that time – what did you understand your responsibilities would be relative to the business?

I'm not asking what changed later. Just going back to 2010, what did you understand you were going to do relative to the business?

ATTORNEY 1: Objection, vague and ambiguous, compound. Can you break it down, Attorney 2? And also could you pinpoint what we're talking about, the timing of this? Could we be clear? You said 2010, and then you also said the time when you were getting ready to start. Could you just be more specific about what time you're talking about?

Q. (By ATTORNEY 2) Do you understand the question?

ATTORNEY 1: Would you like clarification?

THE WITNESS: Could I please have clarification of the question.

Q. (By ATTORNEY 2) Sure. You just told us you were ready to start a business in 2010.

A. Yes, sir.

Q. Put yourself back in 2010. I'm looking for what you were thinking at that point in time, okay. What did you understand – as of the day you signed the partnership agreement, for example, what did you understand your responsibilities were going to be relative to the business?

ATTORNEY 1: Objection, a compound question, vague and ambiguous. You said 2010, and then you also turned around and said, for example, the day you signed the partnership. What point in time are we talking about?

That is a fair request for clarification. When are you talking about? One place, and then you can move on to another time.

ATTORNEY 2: Please answer the question.

ATTORNEY 1: Please break it down.

THE WITNESS: Are you talking about when we signed the partnership agreement?

Q. (By ATTORNEY 2) Yes.

A. Fifty percent responsibility of the business.

Q. Responsibility for what?

A. At that point we were just starting up. The responsibilities that I knew I would have would be writing courses, helping with pushing the business up in the Internet, and being 50 percent fiduciary responsible for that business.

Q. What did you understand G's responsibilities to be?

A. The same.

Q. Were there any responsibilities that you understood one of you would do to the exclusion of the other?

A. No.

ATTORNEY 1: Objection, vague and ambiguous. What do you mean, to the exclusion of the other?

Q. (By ATTORNEY 2) What did you understand your monetary commitments to the business to be?

ATTORNEY 1: Is that a new question, or is that clarification of the prior question? Because I'm really confused right now. Is that part of an explanation of exclusion of the other, or is that a new question? Attorney 2, could you –

ATTORNEY 2: No, I am not going to answer you.

ATTORNEY 1: I'm honestly confused, sir. I can't understand what -

My Crazy Deposition

ATTORNEY 2: Your client is doing fine. She's answering all my questions notwithstanding your comments.
ATTORNEY 1: Thank you.
ATTORNEY 2: I'm not going to answer -
ATTORNEY 1: I was talking.
ATTORNEY 2: – your objections.
ATTORNEY 1: You're making it very hard for the stenographer.
ATTORNEY 2: Let me make my comment. I am not going to respond to you ever.
ATTORNEY 1: You are objecting to me every time.
ATTORNEY 2: No, I am not.
ATTORNEY 1: Can we get clarification. I'm confused. I'm objecting as to vague and ambiguous as to the form of the question. I don't – I don't know what you're talking -are you clarifying the prior question from my prior objection, or are you asking a new question? Come on, why are you making this –
ATTORNEY 2: Again he can make objections. He's entitled to make objections. I have no problem with him objecting all he wants. I'm asking you questions. He makes an objection for the record. You answer the question. That's the process we go through. If you don't understand my question, just tell me, and I will repeat or rephrase the question for you. I am not going to respond to his objections.

Q. So the question for you was, what did you anticipate your monetary commitments to the partnership to be?
ATTORNEY 1: Objection, vague and ambiguous. Are you asking – are you clarifying the prior two questions, or is that a new question?

Can you just answer that, Attorney 2? It's simple. Why are you being hard? You're acting like we're being difficult. It's a simple question, and you can answer it and resolve it in three seconds.
ATTORNEY 2: Please answer my question.
ATTORNEY 1: Okay.
ATTORNEY 2: Please answer my question.
ATTORNEY 1: Or request clarification. You can do that, no problem.

*** During these exchanges I could hear more than one question being asked, so I would try to answer only one of the questions.

THE WITNESS: Could you please clarify the question.
Q. (By ATTORNEY 2) Do you know what the word "monetary" means?
A. Yes, sir, I do.
Q. Do you know what the word "commitment" means?
A. Yes, sir, I do.
Q. So what did you understand your monetary commitments to the partnership to be?
A. Our start-up contribution was a thousand dollars apiece.
Q. And did you understand that was your only monetary contribution?
A. No.
Q. Did you understand you might have other monetary obligations?
A. Yes.
Q. What did you understand those to be?
A. If there was additional start-up costs, we would split the costs of whatever additional costs arose.

My Crazy Deposition

Q. Did you anticipate that you would be hiring someone else to run or operate your business for you as an employee?
A. No.

> ***This question was a detriment to me in court. I should have added "we may have decided to hire in the future", but he kept saying "…only thinking about at this time". In court he said something like "you had no intention of hiring employees". It made it sound like the intention was to stay a "mom and pop" company, and there was no intention to grow the business. I was only talking about that moment in time.

ATTORNEY 1: Objection –
Q. (By ATTORNEY 2) So would you expect –
ATTORNEY 1: – vague and ambiguous as to the time -
ATTORNEY 2: She's already answered the question.
ATTORNEY 1: Are we still talking about the start-up -
ATTORNEY 2: She's already answered the question. She's already answered the question. She obviously understood it. It was very simple. She answered it. I don't care whether you understood it. Next question.
ATTORNEY 1: I would like clarification on the time we were talking about on the questions. Can you say at the start-up or throughout the course, 2010? When are you talking about? Are we still in the start-up phase?
ATTORNEY 2: Are you done?
ATTORNEY 1: I'm just asking. Can you clarify your -

ATTORNEY 2: You've made your objection. No, I am not going to clarify it. You made your objection. Tell me when you're done, and I'll ask the next question.

ATTORNEY 1: It's not like your questions are perfect or something.

ATTORNEY 2: Are you done?

ATTORNEY 1: For the thousands of objections – or thousands of depositions or hundreds of thousands that you said, I'm not iGressed, Attorney 2. Can you be more precise? Can you take smaller steps? Can you clarify your questions?

ATTORNEY 2: Are you done?

ATTORNEY 1: This is basic. Can you -

ATTORNEY 2: Are you done?

ATTORNEY 1: – clarify?

I am done.

ATTORNEY 2: Thank you. Next question.

Q. Was there any point in time where you and G discussed the potential need to hire an employer to work for "My Business"?

A. I do not recall.

Q. Do you have a recollection of ever having a conversation about hiring someone?

ATTORNEY 1: Objection, calls for hearsay testimony. You can answer if you recall.

THE WITNESS: I do not recall.

> ***I was only referring to the startup time frame of the business, and I am not sure if I should have answered for later on or not.

My Crazy Deposition

Q. (By ATTORNEY 2) All right. Let's move a little bit forward to the starting of the business. Did you obtain a business license?
A. Yes.
Q. Who actually obtained the business licenses
A. G.
ATTORNEY 1: Objection. What do you mean by who –
Q. (By ATTORNEY 2) Did you open a bank account?
ATTORNEY 1: Objection, vague and ambiguous. Are we talking partnership or Ms. individually? What are we talking about here?
ATTORNEY 2: I think she knows exactly what she's -
ATTORNEY 1: Well, I don't. Can you -
ATTORNEY 2: It doesn't M.er what –
(Reporter interruption.)

> *** This was early on in the day, and she has already stopped them several times. If the court reporter was frustrated, you can imagine how frustrated I was as well.

ATTORNEY 2: Just make your objections, and then stop talking, and we'll proceed with the answer.
ATTORNEY 1: I'm trying to help you ask questions.
ATTORNEY 2: No, you're not.
ATTORNEY 1: Yes, I am. And I'm trying to keep my client from stumbling into commitments and admissions on the record for questions she doesn't fully understand. So can we be clear? You started to go in that direction, and when you said something like at any time, that would be very helpful -

*** He was right. I am not an attorney, and I did not fully understand how his questioning was leading me down a path I could not go back down. I only had a few hours of prep time and a few videos to watch. With what little time I had, I did the best I could. It felt like I was doing an awful job.

ATTORNEY 2: Have you finished?
ATTORNEY 1: I've not finished.
ATTORNEY 2: Finish your objection.
ATTORNEY 1: Can you please make clarifications moving forward of what time we're in. ATTORNEY 2: That is not an objection. Make your objection.
ATTORNEY 1: Vague and ambiguous -
ATTORNEY 2: Thank you.
ATTORNEY 1: – as to the time of your question, sir.

Q. (By ATTORNEY 2) Did you at any time open a bank account for "My Business"?
A. No.
ATTORNEY 1: Objection as to –
Q. (By ATTORNEY 2) At any point was a bank account opened?
A. Yes.
Q. Who opened the bank account?
A. G.
Q. At what bank?
A. *** *******.
Q. And did you each at the formation of the business just put a thousand dollars in the bank account?
A. No.

Q. At some point did you each put a thousand dollars in that bank account?
A. Not the full amount.
Q. What does that mean?
A. We built up to the thousand dollars.
Q. So over time you each invested a thousand dollars?
A. Correct.
Q. After that initial thousand dollars, to your recollection did either of you ever put more money into the bank account yourselves?
A. I don't recall.
Q. Did the business obtain a taxpayer identification number?
A. It did.
Q. Who obtained the taxpayer identification number?
A. G.
Q. Did the business ever obtain a State of California employment number?
ATTORNEY 1: Objection, vague as to the State of California -
THE WITNESS: I do not recall.
ATTORNEY 1: – employment number.
Q. (By ATTORNEY 2) Did you have a single Computer– meaning only one – that was dedicated to the business?
ATTORNEY 1: Objection, assuming facts not in the record. She's never said at any time that she had a Computer or the partnership had a Computer. So maybe we could start before that and build up to this question.
Q. (By ATTORNEY 2) Please answer the question.
A. I defer to my attorney.

> *** In my mind again I was wondering, "Did he just ask a trick question"? Where was this leading?

ATTORNEY 1: If you – okay. If you understand –

Q. (By ATTORNEY 2) Was there –

ATTORNEY 1: – you can answer. Sorry, go ahead.

Q. (By ATTORNEY 2) Was there at any point in time one Computer dedicated solely to the business?

A. No.

Q. Were there more than one Computers that worked for the business or were used for the business?

A. Yes. We each had our own Computer.

Q. Was there a checkbook for the business?

A. Yes.

Q. Who maintained the checkbook?

A. We each had our own allotted amount of checks to be able to control the checking account.

Q. So you had certain company checks and G had certain company checks?

Correct.
Q. And you each had the authority to pay bills?
ATTORNEY 1: Objection, compound question.
But go ahead and answer.
THE WITNESS: Yes.
Q. (By ATTORNEY 2) When you started the business, how did you plan to do its bookkeeping?
A. All business expenses were put on automatic deposit – withdrawals.
Q. I'm sorry, say that again?
A. All bills were paid by automatic withdrawals.
They were set up for automatic payments to be taken out of the account.
Q. What do you understand the word "bookkeeping" to mean?
A. To keep records.
Q. Of what?
A. Finances or anything deemed necessary by the company.
Q. So at the start of the business, how did you understand its bookkeeping was to be handled?
A. At that time we were using the checking account as our bookkeeping process.
Q. So did you at any point hire a third party bookkeeper?
No.
Q. Did you personally at any time do the bookkeeping for the business?
A. Yes.
Q. And did G at any time do the bookkeeping for the business?
A. Yes.

Q. When you did the bookkeeping, describe for me what you did which you believe constituted bookkeeping? In other words, what did you do that you thought was bookkeeping?
A. Last year when we had the 2014 taxes, we reconciliated all the expenses in order to have the correct tax figures submitted to the – for our taxes.
Q. So it sounds like what you're saying is at the end of the year, you would add up all your revenues and your expenses to give to your accountant?
A. We did not have an accountant.
Q. Well, whoever prepared your tax returns?
A. To whoever prepared our tax returns.
Q. Who did prepare your tax returns each year?
A. For the first several years, it was a gentleman that G was using for her taxes. And the last two years, it's been ****** ******* with *** **** *****.
Q. And why did you change accountants?
I do not know what happened with G's original tax preparer. When she changed her tax person, she requested to take the taxes with her.
Q. As I recall, he died. Does that sound –

> *** I did not ask G if the tax person had passed away, he was an older gentleman, and was planning to stop doing the taxes. I was not aware that he had actually passed away. They brought this up in court to make it look like I had nothing to do with the taxes.

> ATTORNEY 1: Objection. Do you want to testify -

THE WITNESS: I don't know that, sir. I don't know what happened to him.

Q. (By ATTORNEY 2) Was it your understanding that your partnership was to be an equal partnership?

A. Yes.

Q. That you were to divide profits equally?

A. Yes.

Q. Divide decision-making for important decisions, so to speak?

A. All decisions were supposed to be 50/50.

Q. Going back again to the formation of the business, what was your understanding would happen if you disagreed?

A. We would –

ATTORNEY 1: Objection. What do you mean by disagreed? It's such an open-ended question. Can you narrow it down? Disagreed on what? Who disagreed, what? What are you talking about?

ATTORNEY 2: Go ahead. You started to answer before he interrupted your answer.

ATTORNEY 1: Objection, vague and ambiguous. Could you please provide additional clarification as to what you're talking about instead of just saying disagreed? Disagreement between partners? Disagreement with third party vendors? What are we talking about here?

THE WITNESS: I was going to ask for clarification.

Q. (By ATTORNEY 2) If you and G had a disagreement, what would happen?

A. We were going to try to work it out.

Q. That was your understanding when you formed the business as the logical way to proceed, try to work it out?

A. Yes, sir.

Q. Was either of you to have a greater voice than the other in the response –
A. No.
Q. – to any disagreement?
ATTORNEY 1: Let him fully state his question.
THE WITNESS: Sorry.
Q. (By ATTORNEY 2) Did you discuss what would happen in the event of some stalemate; in other words, you tried to work it out and you just couldn't agree?
A. We did not discuss that at the start-up of the business.
Q. As to again your frame of mind at the start-up of the business, what was your understanding of the circumstances under which the business would or could end?
ATTORNEY 1: Objection, vague and ambiguous as to what you mean by business and what you mean by end. Are you talking about the partnership entity itself? Ending the business online? Could you please clarify? I think it's vague and ambiguous and -
THE WITNESS: Could you please clarify the question.
Q. (By ATTORNEY 2) Do you know what I mean by business, the business of "My Business"?
Do you have an understanding what that is?

> ***I was trying to not let this get to me, it was so condescending. It did get to me later, and I think this type of attitude definitely wore me down.

A. Yes, sir.
Q. Do you know what the word "end" means?
A. Yes, sir.
Q. So under what circumstances could the business end?

My Crazy Deposition

ATTORNEY 1: Objection, vague and ambiguous still. Are we talking about the partnership or the online business? Are we talking about the entity of these two -
ATTORNEY 2: Make your objection.
ATTORNEY 1: I did. I'm trying to help you clarify.
ATTORNEY 2: Are you done with your objection?

ATTORNEY 1: That is part of my objection.
ATTORNEY 2: It's not your role to tell me how to ask questions. It's your role to make objections.

Q. He's made an objection. Now you have to answer the question.
A. I felt that the ending – or let me restate my answer. I felt that our partnership agreement addressed how our affairs would be –
Q. I'm not asking what the partnership agreement said. I'm asking your subjective understanding. And it may be the same, and that's okay.
A. It's the same, sir.
Q. Okay. What do you believe – what type of circumstances could result in the end of the business?
ATTORNEY 1: Objection. You're asking her to hypothesize and speculate about something she's not said she actually ever thought about. So maybe –
ATTORNEY 2: Why don't you stop testifying for her. If that's your answer, that could be your answer.
ATTORNEY 1: It's vague as all –
Q. (By ATTORNEY 2) What I'm asking is what your understanding was.
A. At the time of the start-up, I was not thinking of the end.

Q. Okay. That's fine. Did you understand that either of you had the right to end the partnership at any time?
A. Yes.

> *** This is where I should have clarified and said per our partnership contract everything had to be in writing. I was focusing on trying to only answer a question, but this was a hindrance to me in court.

Q. Did you –
ATTORNEY 1: Objection – sorry.
Q. (By ATTORNEY 2) Did you ever make any effort to learn at the start of the business the intricacies of California partnership law?
ATTORNEY 1: Objection, relevancy.
THE WITNESS: I defer to my attorney.
ATTORNEY 1: No, you can answer.
ATTORNEY 2: You can answer.
ATTORNEY 1: I'm sorry, you can answer.
THE WITNESS: No.

> *** This type of question was hard to answer because I had no Idea where he was going with this. I felt the "no" was saying I did nothing to educate myself on partnerships, and I had.

Q. (By ATTORNEY 2) At the formation of the business, did you know what California law provided about the rights of partnerships?
ATTORNEY 1: Objection. This is an absurd line of questioning. You're asking, first of all, the entire body of -

ATTORNEY 2: Make your objection. Stop testifying.

ATTORNEY 1: No. I'm still speaking, sir. I'm still speaking. So if I could finish, then you can say whatever you're saying. It's an absurd question. It's asking for such a broad – it's vague and ambiguous, first of all, as to California law, what aspect of California law. I'm a lawyer; you're a lawyer. We don't know every aspect of California partnership law. What are you talking about? It's an absurd question. It's absolutely irrelevant as to – as to this case -

ATTORNEY 2: Are you finished with your objection?

ATTORNEY 1: – whether or not she understood or – I'm still speaking – or understands California partnership law.

ATTORNEY 2: Answer the question, please.

ATTORNEY 1: What aspects of California partnership law? Maybe a specific area? Like the law in termination? Start-up? Fiduciary duties? What are we talking about here?

ATTORNEY 2: Answer the question, please.

ATTORNEY 1: Vague and ambiguous.

THE WITNESS: I purchased two books that addressed starting up a company. I searched the Internet to try to understand the process so that I could be more familiar on aspects of a partnership.

Q. (By ATTORNEY 2) Is it fair to say that at the time you formed the partnership with G, you felt at some point the business would be hers exclusively?

A. There was a time that when we started the business, I'm ten years older than G, and we did discuss the fact at some point I would probably retire.

Q. So when you started the business, it was your expectation that it was more likely she would end up with the business exclusively than you would end up with the business exclusively? ATTORNEY 1: Objection. That's a compound question. Could you break it down.

THE WITNESS: Could you clarify that question.

ATTORNEY 2: Could you repeat that. It's really just a yes or no question.

ATTORNEY 1: No, it asks for two -

THE WITNESS: It seems like there's more questions.

ATTORNEY 2: No. Listen to the question carefully. (Whereupon the last question "So when you started the business, it was your expectation that it was more likely she would end up with the business exclusively than you would end up with the business exclusively" was read back as requested.)

ATTORNEY 1: That's two questions.

THE WITNESS: There's more than one question, sir. Could you please clarify that question. ATTORNEY 2: Let me try to break that down because I'm just asking a true or false question, yes or no.

Q. Do you agree with me that at the time you formed the business it was your belief that it was more likely she would end up with the business than you would end up with the business? It's a yes or no question.

> ***I should have asked him to ask me a question that left out the "do you agree with me". When he states "do you agree", I did not agree with him.

ATTORNEY 1: It's vague and ambiguous as to what you mean by – objection, as to what you mean by more likely. What do you mean by more likely here? She's going to

die first? What are we talking about here? Would you like further clarification, or can you answer the question?
THE WITNESS: My expectation was not necessarily at some point G would end up with the business. I just was thinking of reality that I was ten years older and at some point I would retire.

> *** Huge mistake on my part, I should have never put it in writing that if I was to retire the business could continue on. Don't be naïve.

Q. (By ATTORNEY 2) And you told her that, right?
ATTORNEY 1: Objection.
THE WITNESS: Yes.
ATTORNEY 1: You're testifying for her.
Q. (By ATTORNEY 2) You told her that in writing, didn't you?
A. No.
Q. Never put that in writing?
A. I did not put those specific words in writing.
ATTORNEY 1: Asked and answered. She just said no.
THE WITNESS: No.
Q. (By ATTORNEY 2) At the time you were starting this business, did you ever – did you expect that it would ever replace your day job?
ATTORNEY 1: Objection. What do you mean by replace and expect and at what time? At the start? Throughout the course of the business? What are we talking about? Could we narrow it in scope of time?
THE WITNESS: Could you clarify that question, please, sir.
ATTORNEY 2: Could you read the question again.

If you listen to the question, you'll see all of his objections are in the question because he doesn't listen very carefully. So just listen to the question. (Whereupon the last question "At the time you were starting this business, did you ever – did you expect that it would ever replace your day job" was read back as requested.)

THE WITNESS: The hopes was that at one point we would be able to run the business full time.

Q. (By ATTORNEY 2) In 2010 what did you earn from your employment at "Employer"?

A. I do not recall.

Q. Best estimate.

A. I do not recall.

Q. More than ten dollars?

ATTORNEY 1: Objection. She's already said she doesn't recall. It's asked and answered. Can we move on?

Q. (By ATTORNEY 2) More than ten dollars?

A. I do not remember the specific amount of money that I earned in 2010.

Q. I understand that, but I'm entitled to your best estimate. And you have an estimate in your head which is more than I know. I don't know if you made ten dollars or ten million dollars, and I'm entitled to your best estimate, whatever that comfort level is. So I'm going to keep narrowing it until you answer that question. Did you make more than ten dollars?

A. I do not know the specific amount of money, and I do not want to estimate on what I made that particular –

Q. So you're telling me you do not know if you made more than ten dollars?

ATTORNEY 1: Objection. You're asking her to speculate.

Q. (By ATTORNEY 2) That's the question in front of you.
A. Yes, I made ten dollars.
Q. Did you make ten million dollars?
A. No, sir.
Q. So now I know it's between ten and ten million. Did you make more than five million dollars?
A. No, sir.
Q. Did you make more than five hundred dollars?
A. Yes, sir.
Q. Okay. So now I know it's between five hundred and whatever I just said. Did you make more than a hundred thousand dollars?
A. I do not know at this time.
Q. Did you make more than fifty thousand dollars?
A. Yes.
Q. Did you make more than two hundred thousand dollars?
A. No.
Q. So in 2010 you earned between fifty and two hundred?
A. Yes.
Q. Did you make more than ******?
A. Yes.
Q. Did you make more than a *******?
A. I do not know.
Q. Did you make more than a ******?
A. I do not know.
Q. So you're only comfortable saying that you earned between ***** and ******?
A. It was not ********.
Q. Yes. So you made more than **** but less than ****?
A. Yes.

Q. And you're not comfortable putting any greater parameters on that?
A. At this moment I do not remember the amount I was making at the time to make that estimate correct.
Q. In 2016 what did you earn at "Employer"?
A. More than a **** and ****.
Q. Less than a *******?
A. I don't remember the exact amount. It was probably close to a ********.
Q. Less than a ***** and *****?
A. Yes.
Q. So something plus or minus a **********.
And is that about your salary for the last four or five years?
ATTORNEY 1: Objection, vague and ambiguous as to what you mean by about her salary.
THE WITNESS: We do receive pay raises every year, but I don't know the exact amounts.
Q. (By ATTORNEY 2) Is that a reasonable approximation of what you've earned in prior years?
A. Yes, sir.
Q. Do you know what G earned at "Employer" in any of the last five years?
A. I have no idea what G earned.
Q. Do you have any reason to believe she earned less than you did?
A. I have no idea what G makes per hour. I have no idea what G makes.
Q. Have you ever discussed your combined earnings?
A. No.
ATTORNEY 1: Objection, hearsay.

Q. (By ATTORNEY 2) But you believe when you formed this business that you would eventually earn enough money from the business that you would not need to work at "Employer"?
A. That was our goal.
ATTORNEY 1: Objection, asked and answered.
Q. (By ATTORNEY 2) I'm only asking your goal. Was that your goal?
A. My goal, yes, sir.
Q. Did G ever describe that that was her goal?

> **** I never thought they would take the position that the business was just a hobby for G, and making money was not why G went into business.

ATTORNEY 1: Objection, calls for hearsay.
You can answer.
THE WITNESS: In the beginning she made it known that she would like to have a successful business and to be able to possibly leave work.
Q. (By ATTORNEY 2) When did she tell you that?
A. I don't remember the exact date. I don't recall. I remember in the time frame of starting up the business, we had a conversation about how we would like to be able to have other opportunities outside of work.
Q. At some point you created a website for the business, right?
A. Yes, sir.
Q. And this was done by this person J?
A. J.

Q. Have you remembered his last name yet?
A. I think I would be close. We would have to go to the records to know the exact.
Q. That's okay. I'm just asking you. If you don't remember –
A. ******? But I don't know that for sure.
ATTORNEY 1: Objection, relevance. Can we just –
Q. (By ATTORNEY 2) Did you acquire a domain name?
A. Yes.
Q. How many domain names did you acquire?
A. One at that time.
Q. What was the domain name?
A. ************.
Q. Who acquired the domain name?
A. I thought of the domain name.
Q. Who acquired it?
A. J.
ATTORNEY 1: Objection. What do you mean -vague and ambiguous as to what you
Q. (By ATTORNEY 2) And do you know what company he bought it from?
ATTORNEY 1: I don't know the – if you don't know, you don't know. If you know, answer. THE WITNESS: I believe it was Vendor.
Q. (By ATTORNEY 2) Do you know how long he acquired it for?
A. It was a year-to-year contract.
Q. Did you have more than one website at any time?
A. Yes.
Q. What were the addresses –
A. I'm sorry, could I retract that statement?

Q. Sure.
A. No.
Q. You only had one?
A. One website.
Q. And what was the web address for that website?
A. ******************.
Q. Are you familiar with Vendor?
A. Yes.
Q. What is Vendor?
A. That is the testing company that "My Business" uses to offer the **** the testing part of our ***** offerings.
Q. So is Vendor a vendor of "My Business"?
A. I do not know that we call him a vendor. He is a company that we hire to supply us a service.
What do you understand a vendor to be?
A. Through "Employer", they have a generalized vendor policy. That may be somebody that offers an educational opportunity or a service or a product. It doesn't necessarily mean a specific
-Q. I would understand a vendor to be a company that provides a service, and you described Vendor as a company that provides a service.
A. Service.
Q. So to me, that's a vendor. But it's not me that's testifying. It's you. So that's why I'm asking, did you consider Vendor to be a vendor of "My Business"? They provided a service, and you paid –
A. They provided a service, so, yes, they were a vendor.
Q. What was your financial arrangements with Vendor when you first hired them?

A. When we first hired them, they charged us **** hundred dollars.

Q. And what did that *** hundred dollars get you?

A. It gave us the opportunity to grow and to allow us to have as many **** taken as we possibly could on that first year.

Q. So, I'm sorry, what were you buying for **** hundred dollars?

A. The ability to allow our customers to take a ****.

Q. Unlimited?

A. The first year was unlimited.

Q. And that's what **** hundred dollars paid for?

A. For the first year.

Q. And then in subsequent years, what was your financial relationship with them or financial arrangement with them?

A. It was – the second year I believe was the same opportunity. And after that, it was the *** hundred dollars plus the cost of each test.

Q. So you paid them a fee based on some number per test?

A. Correct.

Q. How did you find Vendor?

A. We searched the Internet for testing companies, and G discovered Vendor in her search, and they were the closest company to what we both had expectations for for a **** company.

Q. How did the Vendor site work?
Let me back up a minute.
ATTORNEY 1: Objection, calls for a narrative.
(By ATTORNEY 2) If I'm a customer who comes to your site and wants to take a test, it sounds like what you're telling me is I take that test on Vendor?

A. Correct.

My Crazy Deposition

Q. So how does the Vendor site facilitate taking ****?
A. Could you please rephrase that question?
Q. Sure. Let me back up and put more context in it. The e*** class is just on the "My Business" website?
A. The course itself, the text, is actually on the website, our website, because Vendor cannot accommodate all the information on their site. So our course is on our website.
Q. Right. So if I see some course, I can click on it, get the course on your website, and then I presumably have to take a***t to get ***** ****** credit?
A. Correct. So the link from that course is to Vendor. And then to be able to take the ****, you click take a **** on that site.
Q. And then after the **** is finished, I get credit?
A. A certificate.
  Okay. So it's just a link from your website to Vendor. So my question of how it works, it's a link from one website to the other?
A. Correct. It's a link from our website to Vendor.
Q. And the customer is paying whom?
A. *****************.
Q. And how do they do that?
A. Through PayPal.
Q. And do they have to do that before they can link to take the ****?
A. No. You can link to view the course prior to taking the ***.
Q. So at what point does the fee become due and owing?
A. When they're ready to take the ***.
Q. So they can read the *** –
A. They can read –
Q. Hang on. Let me ask the question.

A. I'm sorry.
Q. They can read the *** on your website without having to pay for it?
A. They can read the course content on our website prior to taking the ****.
That's not what I'm asking. They can read the **** on your website without paying for it?
A. Correct.
Q. They only have to pay for if they want to take the ****?
A. Yes.

> **** Looking back I can see he was testing me to see if I would catch when he exchanged words in his questions. He was interchanging two words here and I never caught it. This cost me later.

Q. So if I'm interested in learning about ***** protocols and things, but I don't care about credits, I can read all the information on your website?
A. Correct, for free.
Q. What is G.B.G.?
A. G.B.G. is the second company that "My Business" went with when J moved to Florida.
Q. So it's a web page manager?
A. It's a web company as well, yes.
Q. How long did you work with this J fellow?
A. I don't recall the exact amount of time. It was close to a yearish.
Q. So he created your website –
A. Optimized it.
Q. – hang on – found you –vw

A. I'm sorry.
Q. – an Internet provider, bought you a domain name, took the web page live?
A. We used J's service for the Vendor which hosted the web page. I'm sorry, I've lost my train of thought.
Q. What I'm trying to understand exactly is what J's company did for you. And it sounds like he prepared your website –
A. Correct.
Q. – with all the data which is on your web page, he bought you a domain name, he found a company to host, an Internet provider, to host the web page, and then he took it live?
He did all those things?
A. J owned the hosting company.
Q. Fine.
A. And he optimized ****************.
Q. And that means he puts words on the Internet, you know, what they like to call search engine optimization to drive people to your website?
ATTORNEY 1: Objection. I think you're -no, go ahead.
THE WITNESS: J had a specific service that he offered which was not just words. He was able to do something that organically grew our company within 30 days.
Q. (By ATTORNEY 2) And that's what web developers call search engine optimization, right?
A. J had a specific service he could offer – he was one of the few guys that was able to have an additional optimization process.
Q. At least that was his sales pitch.

Did you ever do anything to know that it was really exclusive to him?

I'm going to tell you

-A. No.

Q. – every search engine guy tells you the same thing. I'm assuming it's probably not exclusive, but I don't know. So do you know why his protocols or his programs were exclusive?

A. I know that J was very good at coding, and that with his coding abilities, he had – I don't know how he did it, but he was able to optimize us within 30 days.

Q. And then he moves away, so you hired G.B.G.?

A. Correct.

Q. And what is G.B.G.?

A. It's the web hosting company.

Q. So what services does G.B.G. or did G.B.G. provide for "My Business"?

A. They host the site which also includes the email, and they – J created a page which our courses were loaded to so that they could be linked to the company, and he maintained that page.

Q. What did G.B.G. cost "My Business"?

A. He was ** dollars an hour.

Q. So you just paid him as you needed him? There was no monthly fee?

A. No. He kept a balance. So he would replenish that balance as we depleted that balance.

Q. Was there some fixed monthly expense for using G.B.G.?

A. No.

Q. So it was pay as you needed the service?
A. Can I change that answer?
There was a monthly hosting fee which was automatically deducted from the bank account.

> *** With flipping between the two companies I was starting to get confused on which company I was answering for, and I should have clarified with each answer.

Q. That's to host the website regardless of whether G.B.G. provides the service?
A. But it was G.B.G.'s hosting site.
Q. Other than the fee you paid them to host your website, was there any other service that company provided "My Business"?
A. For that ** dollars that they kept in their bank, they would load the courses and help with changing anything that needed to be changed on the site itself.
Q. So that's who you would call when you wrote a new course and said, here's the text of the new course, load it for us?
A. Yes.
Q. Anything else they did for you?
ATTORNEY 1: That you recall.
THE WITNESS: Not that I recall.
Q. (By ATTORNEY 2) How did you find G.B.G.?
A. It was a gentleman that G went to church with.

> ***That was what I was told at the time. This also was used against me in court to make it look like I had nothing to do with the company.

Q. That owned the company or that referred you to the company?
A. G went to church with M. from G.B.G., is what I understand.
Q. The man that owned the company?
A. Correct.
Q. What is a S.U.?
A. The S.U. is the company's assigned access to those companies.
Q. How many companies that you worked with had a S.U.?
ATTORNEY 1: Objection, vague and ambiguous. Are you talking third party vendors? Are you talking company – I'm not sure what you mean by that.
Like vendors? Are we talking other companies that utilize PayPal? What are we talking about?
Q. (By ATTORNEY 2) Do you understand what I'm asking?
A. Yes.
Q. Go ahead and answer then.
ATTORNEY 1: Okay.
THE WITNESS: G.B.G., Vendor, PayPal, which is the – how we received our money which is the part that I created. The way the ****** account was set up also had a password that was somehow controlled by -through somehow the way it was set up by ********.
Q. (By ATTORNEY 2) So you've described at least three companies that adopted the concept of a S.U.: G.B.G., PayPal and Vendor. As to G.B.G., whose decision was it to set up a S.U., yours or theirs?
A. The company usually will have one person set it up, set up that S.U. password. ATTORNEY 1: I don't think she –

My Crazy Deposition

Q. (By ATTORNEY 2) That was the company's choice, not – when you say the company, you mean the vendor, not "My Business", right?

A. Yes.

Q. Okay. So in each of those three situations, the vendor – PayPal, G.B.G. or Vendor – they set up the concept of the S.U.?

A. Those companies set up the fact that there is one way to get into that company, correct.

Q. With your accounts for PayPal, G.B.G. and Vendor, did you and G each have your own password?

A. No.

Q. If I asked that question about the three companies, is the answer the same as to all three?

A. Yes.

Q. So you had – you did not each have your own password for PayPal?

A. No.

Q. You did not each have your own password for G.B.G.?

A. Not as a S.U., no.

Q. That's not what I'm asking.
Did you each have a password-linked access to PayPal?
ATTORNEY 1: Objection.
THE WITNESS: Could you please repeat.
ATTORNEY 2: Sure.
ATTORNEY 1: It's a little vague. Can we -
ATTORNEY 2: She's asked me to repeat or rephrase it. I will.

> *** I knew this line of questions was going to be really important, and I was trying not to make a mistake. G had changed all the passwords removing my access to all three of the companies we were dealing with.

Q. As to the "My Business" account with PayPal, did you and G each have separate log-on passwords?
A. No.
Q. So there is just one log-on password?
A. One log-on password for the company.
Q. As to G.B.G., did you and G each have separate log-on passwords?
A. No.
Q. Just one?
A. Just one.
Q. As to Vendor, did you and G each have separate log-on passwords?
A. No.
Q. Just one?
A. Just one.
ATTORNEY 1: When are you thinking about a break? Are you guys good? I'm good, but I just -
THE REPORTER: Can I take one minute, literally one minute?
ATTORNEY 2: Sure.
(Brief recess taken.)

> *** We went to use the restroom, the court reporter told me this was the worst deposition she had done for her part (the typing) of a case.

My Crazy Deposition

She said she had been doing this for a long time. She too could feel the tension in the air.

Q. (By ATTORNEY 2) All right. I want to start with the formation of the business in the spring of 2010 and sort of month to month look at your operations. So to the best you're able to estimate -obviously it's some years later now – how many hours per day or per week were you spending on the business of "My Business" in its initial months – initial month, let's say?
A. I do not recall.
Q. Five or ten? Fifty or a hundred? I mean what's your best estimate?
A. Unless I was able to go back to my records, I cannot give an estimate. I do not recall.
Q. You were still working full time?
A. I was still working full time.
Q. Your kids were obviously six years younger than they are now -
ATTORNEY 1: Objection, relevance.
Q. (By ATTORNEY 2) – right?
A. I defer to my attorney.
ATTORNEY 1: I think the best answer to this, the best evidence is going to be the records themselves. I don't see the reason we're -
ATTORNEY 2: It doesn't M.er what he thinks.
Q. Can you answer my question?
A. I defer to my attorney.
ATTORNEY 1: You can answer if you -
THE WITNESS: Could you please repeat the question.

ATTORNEY 1: – know the answer. (Whereupon the question "Your kids were obviously six years younger than they are now" was read back as requested.)

THE WITNESS: Yes.

Q. (By ATTORNEY 2) They have more activities that you were spending time with them six years ago than you did today?

ATTORNEY 1: Objection, vague and ambiguous as to what you mean by more time.

THE WITNESS: No.

> *** This line of questions was leading in to make it look like there was no way I could be spending time working on the business. This is why having a time card becomes important. I should have had one for each of the different tasks that I had performed in the business. Those time cards would have really helped in court.

Q. (By ATTORNEY 2) Were you spending more than 40 hours per week on "My Business" when the company opened in its first month?

A. Yes.

Q. Describe what you did that took you more than 40 hours per week.

A. I was staying up late and working throughout the day since I was working evening shift. I had more time during the days to be able to focus on writing courses on the initial start-up.

My Crazy Deposition

Q. What I asked you was what you were doing, and the only part of that of what you were doing was writing courses. Is that your primary task in 2010, writing courses?
ATTORNEY 1: Objection. That question calls for a narrative, but I appreciate -
ATTORNEY 2: That was a yes or no question.
Q. Was your only task writing courses? That's what I asked you.
A. In the initial start-up, yes.
Q. And you were spending more than 40 hours a week doing that?
A. I was spending at least 40 hours a week doing that.
Q. For how many weeks did you spend at least 40 hours writing courses?
A. For at least the first year.
Q. So for at least a year you spent at least 40 hours per week?
A. Yes.
Q. How long typically did it take you to write a course?
A. That varied.
ATTORNEY 1: Objection. It's vague and ambiguous.
Q. (By ATTORNEY 2) Well, I understand that, but give me a range.
A. It depended on the length of the course. It really varied.
Q. Well, give me a range.
ATTORNEY 1: She just said it varied. Maybe you can do what you did before and give her projections and -
THE WITNESS: Could you clarify that question.
Q. (By ATTORNEY 2) Sure. Did it take you less than an hour to write a course ever?
A. No.
Q. Did it ever take you more than six months?

A. No.

> ***For this answer I was referring to only the 1st year. I should have clarified what period of time he was addressing.

Q. So you've given me an extreme. Within that extreme, give me an estimate of what the reasonable time it took to write an average course was. I don't know if you did it in a day or a week or a month or three months.
ATTORNEY 1: Objection, vague and ambiguous as to average course. Her definition of average and your definition could vary.
ATTORNEY 2: I don't have one. It's your definition.
ATTORNEY 1: It's vague and ambiguous as to what you mean by writing. Is it research involved in the writing? Is it just the writing? Could we – if you want to break it down in components, that would be helpful, the process, yeah. So if you'd like further clarification, you can request it. Or if you have an answer to his vague question, you can answer that as well.
THE WITNESS: Could you please clarify the question.

Q. (By ATTORNEY 2) Sure. From the very first time a thought popped into your head about a potential course until you had a draft of that course in writing, what was the average time frame it would take you in hours?

A. It depended on the research to start that course, and it depended on how long – how many – how long that course was depended on how long it took and my availability to be able to write on that course.

Q. Absolutely understandable. That's why I'm asking you to give me a range.

ATTORNEY 1: Objection. Again it's a vague and ambiguous question here. She's already said she clearly has difficulty giving you the range. She's answered the question the best she can, but she doesn't want to guess.
So maybe we could, I don't know, talk about the specific courses. Would that help? I don't know. THE WITNESS: I don't know the amount of time for each course it took.
Q. (By ATTORNEY 2) I'm not asking for each course. I'm asking for an average.
A. Each course was a different amount of units, and it took a different amount of time for each course to do research and write that course.

> *** This is why I say it is important to keep a time card. I used to think of the time I had spent on my courses in days or weeks, not hours. I was sitting there wishing I had a calculator to have a better idea of the hours I had spent on each course. They took months to write, I was not prepared for this line of questioning. It is hard to try to add numbers in your head while you are paying attention to questions. The questions never stop.

Q. Did you ever – starting from the concept in your head until the draft is on paper, including all your research and how much editing you did, did you ever prepare a course in less than 20 hours?
A. No.
Q. Did you ever prepare one in less than 40 hours?
A. No.

Q. Did you ever prepare one in less than a hundred hours?
A. Yes.
Q. Did you ever do one that took you two hundred hours?
A. I don't know.
Q. Did you ever take one that took you five hundred hours?
A. I do not recall.
Q. So it may have been as much as five hundred hours for a course?
A. Yes.
Q. How many courses did you do work on that you think may have taken you five hundred hours to prepare?
A. I do not recall.
Q. Can you name one that you ever wrote that took you five hundred hours?
A. I do not recall.
Q. Can you name one that you believe ever took you two hundred hours?
A. Yes.
Q. Please do.
A. ****.
Q. ****?
A. *****.
Q. *******?
A. A minimum of two hundred hours.

> ****I should not have answered this question, I should have stuck with I do not recall. I did say minimum, but it took months to write this course.

Q. I'm just making sure I understood the word.
A. *****.

Q. ******?
A. *****.
ATTORNEY 1: Wait until he's done talking.
Q. (By ATTORNEY 2) Any others that you can think of that took you more than two hundred hours?
A. I do not recall.
Q. And that's the time you are researching whatever information you need and the drafting of the course itself?
A. Correct.
Q. Did you ever prepare a course that took less than fifty hours?
A. I do not recall.
Q. Do you believe you did?
A. It was over a period of time. I don't know.
Q. How many courses do you believe you wrote in the five years?
A. Fifteen.
Q. How many of those are you able to name right now?
A. Off the top of my head?
Q. Yes.
A. I could not name them all.
Q. How many of them could you name?
A. I don't know.
Q. Please give me your best shot.
ATTORNEY 1: Would paper help?
THE WITNESS: Yes, please.

> *** I have no Idea why I could not name off my courses easier. It seemed like naming off Santa's reindeer, I should have gone through them before starting this day. I was embarrassed to

> blank out on the names. In some cases what I started out with was not the final name of the course, and I did not want to be wrong.

ATTORNEY 1: Objection as to relevance, but -
THE WITNESS: *****.
ATTORNEY 1: – it's your time.
THE WITNESS: ****** – I may be not exact on the names.
ATTORNEY 1: Why don't you write them all and then list them.
ATTORNEY 2: That's fine, yeah. Just take a second and write them down. We'll go off the record and let you write them down. (Discussion was held off the record from 10:42 a.m. to 10:45 a.m.)

> ***I was sitting there thinking how ridiculous this was not to recall the names. This stressed me out even more. I did not get that much time. The recorder thought we were still off the record. It was approximately less than a minute.

Q. (By ATTORNEY 2) Ms., we just discussed these courses off the record, and, my fault, I didn't know the court reporter wasn't writing down what I said. So I just want to summarize what we talked about. You've identified two, four, seven courses that you've just told me what they were off the record. And as to each of them, you said you didn't really remember how much time you spent preparing them because it's been too long. But the courses are two on *****e, one on *****, one called the *******, one called ***** – which you did not recall what the letters stood for

My Crazy Deposition

– one on ***** and one on E. Is that a correct summary of what we talked about off the record?

A. Those are the courses that I can remember at this time – the names of the courses that I wrote at this time, correct.

Q. You didn't remember any other courses, and you didn't remember how much time you spent on any of them, agreed?

A. There are more courses. I do not remember the amount of time spent on those courses, correct.

Q. In the first couple months the business was operating back in 2010 when you told me you were spending more than 40 hours a week on the business of "My Business", how much time would you spend relative to marketing the business of "My Business", if any?

ATTORNEY 1: Objection, vague and ambiguous as to marketing. If you'd like clarification, of course, but if you understand his question, by all means and – yeah.

THE WITNESS: I'm sorry, could you please repeat that question.

Q. (By ATTORNEY 2) How much time did you spend on marketing the business of "My Business"?

A. I do not recall the amount of time I was spending on marketing. But I was creating fliers and distributing fliers at that time.

Just answer the first part, and then I'm going to ask you what that consisted of.

A. Okay.

Q. So within your 40 hours is marketing time, but you don't remember how much of it was marketing; is that fair?

A. Correct.

Q. And then what did you do that you are saying constituted the part of the marketing?

A. So I created fliers and passed out fliers when the opportunity arose, not only to ***** but to the **** staff as well as ***** staff. And I spent a lot of time that first year with J understanding the concept of the hit words. So working on hit words with him. I spent a lot of time trying to understand that process, and adding hit words when the opportunity arose.

Q. Hit words meaning things behind the code of your website to get you –

A. Correct.

Q. – more hits on your website?

A. Correct.

Q. What is ****?

A. *******.

Q. Now, the tests that are available on your website, they're available to people other than *****, right?

A. Correct.

Q. So you prepared fliers, fliers for the people you work with at "Employer"?

A. Yes.

Q. Did you ever distribute fliers other than to people you work with at "Employer"?

A. Yes.

Q. To whom did you distribute fliers beyond the "Employer" facilities?

A. I sent out mailings to multiple large hospitals trying to solicit more customers. I actually through the – through our company, we purchased the California **** list of ****

My Crazy Deposition

that are within California, and I also purchased the one through Texas, and I sent over 250 mailings to Texas *****.

Q. Did you ever personally present any, let's say, sales talks to groups of nurses in 2010?

A. Not in –

ATTORNEY 1: Objection, vague and ambiguous as to what you mean by sales talks. But if you understand, you can answer his question.

THE WITNESS: Not in 2010.

(By ATTORNEY 2) Did you do that in subsequent years?

A. Yes.

Q. How many such sales talks did you present?

> ***This question was one he was developing for court. I never saw how he was going to use this while he was asking the questions. Always insist to finish your answers.

A. We had a conference in –

Q. No. Just you personally. I'm not asking about "My Business". I'm asking about you.

A. Two.

Q. And when and where were they?

A. In Las Vegas.

Q. Did you provide any in-services?

A. No.

> *** What I should have said we were a company and would not have been educating at an in-service, it would have been for advertising. We did not put on educational in-service.

ATTORNEY 1: Objection – well, it's gone.

Q. (By ATTORNEY 2) Did you attend any meetings of **** staffs at other ***** intended for the promotion of the "My Business" business?

A. No. I focused almost all my time on Internet -in the beginning I focused on mailings to see how many nurses would respond with mailings.

Q. What result did you get from those?

A. Not very many.

Q. You mailed 250 brochures or something to –

A. Brochures, business cards.

Q. – the people in Texas.
Did any of them ever take a ****?

A. Only a few.

Q. What's a few to the best of your recollection?

> ***Be very careful putting exact numbers, unless you truly know that number. The other attorney will manipulate those numbers in court.

A. I don't remember the exact number, but it was less than ten.

Q. Did you ever attend any meetings with any of the vendors who were providing services to "My Business"?
ATTORNEY 1: Objection, vague and ambiguous as to what you mean by attend meetings. Does that include phone conferences and things like that? Or actually go to a physical location?
Do you understand the question?
THE WITNESS: Could you clarify the question, please.

Q. (By ATTORNEY 2) Do you know what the word "attend" means?

A. Yes.
Q. Do you know what the word "meeting" means?

> ***He must know how irritating this becomes. I knew I was not supposed to answer vague questions, and I was trying to follow my attorney's lead.

A. Yes.
Q. Did you ever attend a meeting?
A. Yes.
Q. With whom did you attend a meeting?
A. M. with G.B.G..
Q. Is that the only vendor with whom you ever personally attended a meeting?
A. I did phone meetings.
I'm just asking you personally attending.
A. Personally at a meeting?
Q. Yes.
A. J. I spent a lot of time in meetings with J, with M., G.B.G.. I've been – well, with M., yes.
Q. So from your answers, my impression is that if I expanded my question to the rest of calendar year 2010 – because I started by asking just the spring – your answer isn't probably going to change in the winter or fall of 2010; is that fair?
ATTORNEY 1: Objection. Are you going to testify?
THE WITNESS: I would need to say I did not -
ATTORNEY 1: Is that a question?
THE WITNESS: If we're talking only in the spring, then M. wasn't around in the spring.

Q. (By ATTORNEY 2) Your question is about how many hours you spent and what you were doing. Did that change any in the fall and summer of 2010?

ATTORNEY 1: Objection, vague as to change.

What are we talking about, change? Like in the amount? The number? The people themselves? What are you talking about? Are we talking about amount? If it's the number, just say number. If we're talking about the people, say people. And change to what degree?

ATTORNEY 2: Are you done?

ATTORNEY 1: I am done.

ATTORNEY 2: Answer the question, please.

ATTORNEY 1: Do you understand the question, or would you like more clarification from Attorney 2?

THE WITNESS: So I need to clarify my answers. I understood you to ask me vendors. Not all the vendors were in the spring of 2010. So I'm not –

> ***This was very hard because I had already answered for 2010, and the questions he asked were from later in the business. He was purposefully manipulating the dates. We were hours into this deposition, and we are still on 2010. Very few of these last answers were from that year.

Q. (By ATTORNEY 2) You corrected that, I understand.
A. – answering these questions based on 2010.
Q. What I'm asking you now – you've answered my questions about the quantity of time you spent in the first couple months in the spring of 2010 and what you were doing

My Crazy Deposition

vis-a-vis marketing, writing courses. What I'm asking now is, if I broaden my question to the summer and fall of 2010, are your answers any different?
ATTORNEY 1: Objection, vague and ambiguous. Different in what way? I mean what are you asking?
THE WITNESS: So I need to stop and clarify my answer. If we were talking only about 2010, then I have not answered correctly.
I thought we were talking over – when we're talking vendors, I thought over the entirety of the business, because not all vendors were in the spring of 2010.

> ***I tried to clarify here that I did not realize we were only talking about the first year of business. I was also thinking, "I am never getting out of here".

Q. (By ATTORNEY 2) Okay. Other than that, is the rest of your answer accurate?
A. Could you please clarify what you mean, other than that.

> ***I caught this one. These types of his answers became my answers, even though I did not say it. Be aware of this.

Q. I asked you questions. How many hours did you spend; you answered that. I asked you what you spent your time on; you answered that. I asked you what you did in marketing efforts; you answered that. As to those items, did you spend any different quantities of time in the summer of 2010 than you did in the spring of 2010?

105

ATTORNEY 1: Objection. That was a compound question. How can she answer the question? You've listed so many different things. Can you just please -

ATTORNEY 2: I can go back and spend another 20 minutes and go over it again. I assume your answer is no different. So I -

ATTORNEY 1: Attorney 2, please stop cutting me off when I'm talking.

ATTORNEY 2: Will you let me ask the question, and then you can object.

ATTORNEY 1: I did object.

ATTORNEY 2: Then you objected. And let me ask the next question.

ATTORNEY 1: You're out of control. Can you be reasonable? Just take it down a notch, sir.

Q. (By ATTORNEY 2) H, here's where we are.

ATTORNEY 1: Why don't we take a break.

ATTORNEY 2: Let me just ask the question.

Q. I can go back and ask all those questions again for the next month, and you can answer them all again. My assumption is your answer is not any different. So that's why I'm asking one question, are your answers any different?

And if you tell me they're not any different, I'll move on. If you tell me your answers would be different or you want to go through them all again, I'll be glad to do that. But I don't think your answers are any different in the summer than it was in the spring. ATTORNEY 1: I'm going to object. The question is compound. You're asking about months, seasons in different years.

ATTORNEY 2: No, I'm not.

ATTORNEY 1: If you want to ask her about -

ATTORNEY 2: No, I'm not.

ATTORNEY 1: – each period of time -

ATTORNEY 2: He just makes things up.

ATTORNEY 1: No, I don't.

ATTORNEY 2: Has nothing to do with what I asked.

ATTORNEY 1: She got confused – Attorney 2, she was confused by your question and answered the question one way because she didn't know the time periods you were talking about. So it's really important for the record and for us and for my client to understand what the heck you're talking about, okay? Break it down. There's no reason to get upset, Attorney 2, okay? I understand it's Thursday and, you know, you'd probably like to be doing something else. But let's just take it down a notch, let's not talk over each other, and let's ask the questions point by point.

ATTORNEY 2: Are you done?

ATTORNEY 1: I could go on if you'd like.

ATTORNEY 2: Are you done?

ATTORNEY 1: I can go on if you would like to hear more. I'm trying to keep it -

ATTORNEY 2: Please answer the question.

ATTORNEY 1: I'm still talking.

Would you like clarification, or can you answer the question? He has the duty to provide you a clear question, and you have every right to ask for a clear question, H. If you want clarification, you can. You're not required to answer a question that you don't understand or encompasses broader than you can actually answer in a sentence. So, yeah, if you understand the question or if you'd like clarification, answer it or ask for clarification.

Q. (By ATTORNEY 2) Do you understand what I'm asking you?

> ***These exchanges made it more and more difficult as the day went on.

A. Sir, could you please clarify the question.
Q. Okay. I asked you earlier in the first month the company was in business how many hours per week you worked on the business of the company. You answered that. So now let me ask the next question. In May of 2010, how many hours per week did you spend on the business of the company?
A. In May of 2010, I do not recall.
Q. So you recall very vividly that in April you spent more than 40 hours per week, and you don't have any recollection of May?
ATTORNEY 1: Objection, asked and answered. I mean she's said that.
You want to keep harassing her? If you don't like her answer, so what? But she's answered the question. Go on to your next question. God.
Q. (By ATTORNEY 2) Please answer.
ATTORNEY 1: Asked and answered. Please go on.
ATTORNEY 2: Asked and answered is not an objection. Again he can make his record. ATTORNEY 1: You keep –
ATTORNEY 2: You still have to -
THE WITNESS: I do not know the exact amount of hours that I worked in May. I know that I was at least working 40 hours a week.
ATTORNEY 2: Fine. That's all I asked.
Q. And so it's the same as in April, right?

And if I asked you that question in June, is the answer approximately the same?

A. Yes.

Q. And if I asked you that question in July, is your answer approximately the same?

A. Yes.

Q. And if I asked you that question about August, is your answer approximately the same?

A. Yes.

Q. And in September?

A. Yes.

Q. And in October?

A. Yes.

Q. And in November?

A. Yes.

Q. And in December?

A. Yes.

Q. That's why I tried to ask you in one question, did it change the rest of the year, because I assumed your answer was exactly what you told me. I just wanted to hear you say it. But he wants to take 20 minutes to do it so that at the end of the day he can say we're done with our time. That's why we're going to have a fight over this in front of the judge later. So let me go on to the next question. And if you want to do it week by week, I can do that. If you want to summarize over a year, that's fine. It's up to you. So as to your marketing efforts, you told me about the marketing efforts you did starting in the spring of 2010. Would your answers be the same in the fall?

Would your answers be the same in the summer?

A. That's why I was trying to clarify my answer to the marketing. In April of 2010 – I misunderstood the question. Marketing in April, we didn't do that much marketing in April of 2010 because we were building the business. Marketing truly didn't start until – our website wasn't even up until October.

> ***This gave me the opportunity to clarify my answer for 2010. However, he could have used any answer from before. I would have had the burden to find this answer from this deposition for the court. However, I was never able to do that.

Q. So what marketing were you doing in April, May, June, July, August –
A. That's why I needed to clarify my answer, sir.
I didn't understand you were asking me -
ATTORNEY 1: Let him finish.
THE WITNESS: I'm sorry.
Q. (By ATTORNEY 2) So what marketing did you do from April through September?
ATTORNEY 1: Objection, vague and ambiguous. Can we narrow it to a time – more narrow time or something? And vague as to marketing. What are we talking about? The marketing she did at the start-up? There's different things. Her definition of marketing is obviously possibly different than yours. So can we clarify what you're talking about rather than just hitting this with a big shotgun approach?
ATTORNEY 2: Please answer the question.

ATTORNEY 1: If you understand, you can answer. If you'd like more clarification, by all means ask.

THE WITNESS: Our business was not up and running in April, May, June, July or August.

Q. (By ATTORNEY 2) So did you do any marketing?

A. There was no marketing then during those months.

Q. Did you prepare any marketing materials to be used after the website went live prior to the website going live?

A. I did prepare business cards.

Q. And that's the only thing you did which constitutes marketing of any kind?

ATTORNEY 1: Objection. You're mischaracterizing what she said. She said that -

***Attorney A is trying to address how he could mischaracterize what I have said in court.

ATTORNEY 2: Why don't you stop testifying for her.

ATTORNEY 1: Why don't you stop testifying, Attorney 2.

Q. (By ATTORNEY 2) Is preparing business cards the only marketing you did prior to the website going live?

A. Yes.

Q. The fliers you sent to people in Texas, when did they go out to the best of your recollection?

A. Sometime during 2011.

Q. The marketing fliers you gave to people at "Employer", when did they go out to the best of your recollection?

A. 2011.

Q. At any time ever, did you and G ever discuss the possibility of hiring someone else to work for "My Business"?

ATTORNEY 1: Objection, any time ever? Can you please keep it in the narrow scope of time. It's such a broad time. Go ahead, answer if you feel like you can answer his question. Or if you want more clarification, by all means.
THE WITNESS: I do not recall the dates. There was discussion at some point I recall around the possibility if our business grew big enough, that we may need to elicit help.

Q. (By ATTORNEY 2) So it was not a conversation about hiring someone at the present time; just the potential of maybe hiring someone in the future?
A. Correct.
Q. And do you have any recollection of when that conversation took place?
A. I do not recall.
Q. Was it only one conversation?
A. I do not recall.
Q. When you would write a course which you were writing with the expectation of it being published by "My Business", what would you do with the written course materials after you finished them?

> ***This was one of the components I needed to provide ownership of my courses, and he was fishing to see if I had this material. I did, I had kept everything.

ATTORNEY 1: Objection, vague as to what would you do with them after. What do you mean by that? Like burn them? Post them? I don't know what you mean.
Q. (By ATTORNEY 2) You can answer –
ATTORNEY 1: Could you please clarify that?
I would like clarification, Attorney 2.

My Crazy Deposition

Q. (By ATTORNEY 2) What would you do with them?
A. I've saved them.
Q. What did you do with them – well, tell me all the steps you would take between finish writing a draft and getting it live online.

> ***He asked two questions, he could use the answer for either one.

ATTORNEY 1: Objection, calls for a narrative. Answer if you'd like.
THE WITNESS: Could I please have a moment to be able to write down the steps to make sure that I don't miss anything?
Q. (By ATTORNEY 2) This is an oral deposition. I'm entitled to your oral testimony. If you don't remember something, that's okay. That's part of the testimony. It's my risk if you don't remember things.
A. To the best of my knowledge, I remember that my first step would be to research a course, create a draft, go back during that draft to see if I could find any other course material that could possibly fit my course or maybe morph my course a little bit, depending on if I decided to change the direction of how I was creating it. Once the course was created, our agreement in the beginning was that G's *****, C, would edit the course.
Q. So the starting point after you finished writing is you would give it to C?
A. After the course was written, we would give it to C.
Q. Okay.
A. C would edit the course; the changes would be made. During this process, you would have to go to Vendor. It's a

pretty lengthy process to set the website up for preloading that *****.
Q. That's farther ahead than what I'm asking.
A. I thought you wanted to know the process.
Q. I just want to know, between the point in time when you finish your written draft and it goes live on online, what steps are in that process?

So step number one is you give it to C to edit, right?
A. Step number one would be researching the course.
Q. I'm past that. I'm saying starting with when it's finished writing.
A. Oh, finished writing.
Q. So you had finished writing it. What do you then do?
A. Submit it to C for editing.
Q. Does anyone edit other than C?
A. The agreement was C.
Q. You said the agreement. What does that mean?
A. When we started the business, the agreement was C would be editing the courses.
Q. Did that change at some point?
A. At some point it did.
Q. When did it change to the best of your recollection?
A. When I received my ****** back and G had wrote WTF on my course, I asked, what that was about, and she said she had edited the course. And at that time it was addressed that G was not supposed to be editing the courses. And our agreement at that time would be that I would submit my courses to AA, and she would edit my courses.
Q. So to your knowledge, the first time G had edited one of your courses was the ********?

A. Correct.

> ***What I should have added was G was not to be editing my courses, and it was against our agreement. This was one of the things we were fighting about in court.

Q. When was that?
A. Sometime during 2013.
ATTORNEY 1: Can we get a break in the next five or ten?
ATTORNEY 2: Sure, we can take a break.
(Recess taken from 11:05 a.m. to 11:15 a.m.)

> ***The room kept getting warmer, and I had to ask for additional water.

Q. (By ATTORNEY 2) Ms. Hu, to your recollection, at some point did anyone other than C begin editing your tests – yeah, tests I guess?
A. Sir, I'm not *****.
Q. I'm sorry.
A. That's okay.
Q. I have many times confused you with my secretary because her name was H **.
A. I know. I know.
Q. So I've started to type her name on pleadings in this case many times. So I apologize. You were telling me that you gave the test to C and he edited them.
Did anyone else to your knowledge ever edit your tests?
A. A edited my courses.
Q. How many times?
A. Including wound care, twice.

Q. What was the other course that she edited?
A. ****.
Q. And what's her last name?
A. **, *-*- —
Q. *?
A. *-*-*-*.
Q. Anyone else you're aware of that edited tests?
A. Not that I am aware of.
Q. Do you know anyone that edited the tests that G wrote?
A. I thought it was C editing G's courses.
Q. Anyone else?
A. Not to my knowledge.
Q. Didn't "My Business" ask M to edit your courses?
A. I did not ask M to edit my courses.
Q. Are you aware that he was doing so?
A. No.
Q. Are you aware that he was editing G's courses?
A. No.
Q. Is my question the first time you've ever heard that?
A. Yes.
Q. Do you have any estimate of the quantity of time it would take C to edit your courses?
A. I have no idea.
ATTORNEY 1: Objection. Objection, speculation. She's not personal knowledge necessarily of how much time C would take to edit that course.
Q. (By ATTORNEY 2) How would you advise your customers or your potential customers that a new course was put online?
ATTORNEY 1: Objection, vague as to advise.

What are we talking about? Market? Notify? Do you understand what he's talking about? If you do, you can answer. If you'd like more clarification, it's up to you.

THE WITNESS: I would post on Marketing. We had in the past – there is a feature of Vendor; send those courses out to our existing customers.

Q. (By ATTORNEY 2) The equivalent of an email blast –
A. Correct.
Q. – to everyone in your database?
A. Correct. Those are the main ways that I would advertise those courses.
Q. And when you say I, do you mean "My Business"? Is that something you did independent of "My Business"?
A. Not independent of "My Business", no.
Q. Okay.
A. Once the course was posted, I would be – either I or G would send out a mass email advertising those courses.
Q. Why was there a need to edit your courses?
A. There's a need to edit all courses.

ATTORNEY 1: Objection, relevance. God.

Q. (By ATTORNEY 2) Why is there a need to edit G's courses?
A. The agreement was in the beginning that our courses would be edited before we posted them on the website.
Q. Makes sense. The more eyes looking at something, the better?
A. I would only recommend professional editors to edit our courses, and that was the agreement, that our courses would be edited.

> ***I should have been more careful, and clearly stated G was not to be the one editing courses. The initial agreement stated C was to do the editing.

Q. Is it your understanding that your courses were being edited for grammar, punctuation, spelling, as opposed to content?
ATTORNEY 1: Objection, relevance.
THE WITNESS: Courses were being edited for grammar.
Q. (By ATTORNEY 2) Punctuation?
A. Correct.
Q. Spelling?
A. Correct.
Q. The concept wasn't that the editors were changing the content of the course?
A. Editors were not to be changing the course content.
Q. Isn't it true that you admitted that your spelling is not very good?

> ***This is the reason I say never tell the person(s) you are going into business with your weakness. I should have never told G that I was not very good with spelling, and my grammar was weak. I passed my college English courses; I just knew English is not my strongest subject. However, I am very strong in content. Grammar and spelling had nothing to do with the case; it was just used to make me angry. It is much harder to think when you get upset. He used that against me.

My Crazy Deposition

ATTORNEY 1: Objection, relevance. This is – what are you doing, harassing my client about her spelling? What's the relevance? Can you explain what the relevance is, Mr. Price?

Q. (By ATTORNEY 2) Answer the question.
ATTORNEY 1: Could you proffer up the relevance?
THE WITNESS: Spelling was not specifically addressed.

Q. (By ATTORNEY 2) That's not my question.
Didn't you admit that you were not very good at spelling?

A. Yes.

Q. And didn't you admit that your grammar was not that good?

A. Yes.

Q. And didn't you admit that your punctuation wasn't that good?

A. I don't remember specifically saying punctuation.

Q. And you welcomed CH's editing of your grammar, spelling and punctuation?

A. The expectation was our courses were to be edited before being posted on the Internet.

Q. And as you sit here today, do you know the difference between an adjective and an adverb?
ATTORNEY 1: Objection, relevance. This is harassing my client.

> ***This really made me angry realizing someone can be low enough to try to humiliate me. The worst part was the answers I wanted to give are answers you are not supposed to say. Then I could not think of what I wanted to say. This attempt at humiliation really affects

one's thought process. Then I thought, "If I do not give a dictionary type answer, will I look worse"? Then I could not think. I realized later on, if this is all they have, then he must think my case is pretty strong.

ATTORNEY 2: It's a yes or no question.
ATTORNEY 1: Do you know what -
ATTORNEY 2: It's a yes or no question.

Q. Do you know the difference –
ATTORNEY 1: I would like you to proffer up how this is reasonably calculated to lead to the discovery of admissible facts. Could you do that, Attorney 2? Tell me why this is -
ATTORNEY 2: He's entitled to make objections.
ATTORNEY 1: Yes, I am.
ATTORNEY 2: He's made an objection.
ATTORNEY 1: This is terrible and harassing my client.

***It truly was.

Q. (By ATTORNEY 2) I'm asking you if you know the difference between an adjective and an adverb.
ATTORNEY 1: Do you know the difference between a participle and a predicate? No. If you would like to answer that question, you can. If you would like more clarification by what an adjective is or what an adverb is, you can ask him that. It's a meaningless question and a harassing question, Attorney 2. Shame on you, sir.
ATTORNEY 2: It's a yes or no question.
THE WITNESS: Yes, I do. And if I needed clarification, I could always Google it.

My Crazy Deposition

Q. (By ATTORNEY 2) What is the difference between an adjective and adverb?
ATTORNEY 1: Awful.
THE WITNESS: I knew that was coming.

> ***At this time I wished I had done a quick run through of grammar definitions before deposition to keep them fresh in my mind, but who knew there was going to be an English test, and he would stoop this low?

ATTORNEY 1: Of course, it was.
THE WITNESS: An adverb is an action word. An adjective, I'm drawing a blank on. But I have learned what an adjective is and could easily Google it if I'm blank on how I wanted to use it in a sentence.

> *** I wish I had said "I do not recall", and when he continued to hammer me I should have said "I have given my answer". I felt this had nothing to do with why we were going to court, and I should not have allowed them to go to this level.

Q. (By ATTORNEY 2) In your conversations with G, did you acknowledge that her knowledge of ****** details was greater than yours?
A. Absolutely not.

> ***He threw the other question in just to upset me, so I would answer this question wrong.

> This was a good maneuver on his part, but it did not work this time.

Q. Were you ever able to determine whose courses were more popular online, the ones you wrote or the ones she wrote?
A. I did not focus on that aspect of the courses.
I was busy focusing on growing the business.

> ***Right here is why they claimed I did not have any idea what was going on with the business. I was shocked that this small detail was used against me in the way it was. I was not wasting my time on seeing whose courses were taken more often, but G was. I used that time to grow the business over 60% every year. In the end, because G was able to advertise the course, and it was about 50/50 up to the point, I was locked out. I had printed out the information from the prior year; I just had not taken the time to look at it. I did look at it and compared the courses after I was locked out of the business, and was preparing for court.

Q. As you sit here today, do you know how many people, for example, took your courses and how many people took hers?
A. No.
Q. Do you have any idea about that?
A. Not over the last year. I haven't had access to the account.
Q. Ever, ever.
A. I never looked that up, no.

ATTORNEY 1: I move to strike the last three questions and answers to that. Please put that in the record.

*** This was another maneuver for court.

Q. (By ATTORNEY 2) As you moved into subsequent years – 2012, '13, '14 – who was responsible for the bookkeeping of the partnership?
A. We both were.
Q. What did you do incident to responsibilities you considered to be bookkeeping?

***I do not know if he realized what he had said, but I was not going to answer this question in this format.

A. Could you clarify that question, please.
Q. No, I can't. I'm asking what you did that you understood to be bookkeeping?
ATTORNEY 1: Objection, vague and ambiguous as to your question. Can you please explain it.
Q. (By ATTORNEY 2) What does bookkeeping mean?
A. That means we keep track of the funds that are in the –

***At least say you want to finish your answer. If he could not manipulate my answer to be what he wanted, he would stop me from answering.

Q. Okay. What did you do that you thought constituted bookkeeping?
A. I verified at the end of the year the amounts that were coming through PayPal. I always ran the numbers and looked at what was end-year numbers for the accountant.

Q. And what did you understand G did relative to bookkeeping?
A. The same things.
Q. So in your mind you were doing exactly the same things she was doing?
A. Our fiduciary responsibilities were 50/50 –
Q. I understand that.
A. – to monitor the business.
Q. I'm not asking what your responsibilities were. I'm asking what you actually did.
ATTORNEY 1: Can you allow her to finish her sentence, please.
Q. (By ATTORNEY 2) I'm sorry. Were you finished? I thought you were finished.
A. I don't know exactly what G was doing all the time when it came to the fiduciary responsibilities of the company.
Q. Are you aware of anything relative to bookkeeping – because I'm only talking about bookkeeping now – that you did that she did not do or that she did that you did not do?
ATTORNEY 1: Objection, that's a compound question. Can you break it down, please.
THE WITNESS: Could you please clarify the question.
Q. (By ATTORNEY 2) Sure. Are you aware of any bookkeeping tasks that you ever undertook about "My Business" that G did not?
A. I constantly monitored the PayPal account and made sure that those figures were always correct.
Q. And is it your testimony you know that she did not do that?

A. I believe that she would be doing that because we're 50/50 responsible for monitoring all accounts.

> ***Attorney 2 was talking over me.

ATTORNEY 1: Could you allow her to answer?

Q. (By ATTORNEY 2) What I'm asking is only your knowledge of things you believe you did that she did not do. Are you aware of anything relative to bookkeeping that you did that she did not do?

A. Sir, I believe there's more than one statement in there, and I can't answer all of them with just one answer.

> ***He was a very fast speaker, and I should have been more consistent on slowing down. It is really hard when you just want this over, and you are thinking "If I just answer the questions, I can get out of here". I was already feeling like I had been there all day.

Q. It's a very, very narrow, simple question.

> ***It was not, these were all things that were used in court, and my answers were manipulated.

Are you aware of any tasks, any whatsoever, that you undertook about bookkeeping for "My Business" that G did not undertake?

A. I believe we both did things equally.

Q. Are you aware of any tasks that she undertook that you did not undertake?

A. In regards to bookkeeping, no.

Q. Who paid the bills?

A. They were automatic direct payment from the bank account. We set them up so they were automatically paid.
Q. One hundred percent of your bills?
A. Except for "vendor".

> ***This was a company whose name I am changing to vendor.

Q. So it is your belief that G never wrote any checks for business expenses?
ATTORNEY 1: Objection. The question calls for speculation. She doesn't have intricate knowledge of everything that G had done.
ATTORNEY 2: I don't think she'd want to admit to that.

> ***What I should have said was, "I do not live with G in their house, and I do not know what they do there."

ATTORNEY 1: That's okay. I don't – that's okay. The objection is -
Do you understand the question?
THE WITNESS: Yes.
ATTORNEY 1: Again she doesn't -
ATTORNEY 2: Answer it.
ATTORNEY 1: – have personal knowledge of everything -
ATTORNEY 2: Let her answer. She just told me she -
THE WITNESS: Could you please repeat the question though.
ATTORNEY 2: Could you repeat the question.

(Whereupon the last question "So it is your belief that G never wrote any checks for business expenses" was read back as requested.)

THE WITNESS: Could you please clarify that question.

Q. (By ATTORNEY 2) To your knowledge, did G ever write any checks to pay business expenses?

A. Yes.

Q. Are you aware of any of your business vendors who did not even know you?

ATTORNEY 1: Objection -

THE WITNESS: No.

ATTORNEY 1: – vague and ambiguous.

THE WITNESS: I'm sorry.

> ***I realized I answered before I let my attorney finish.

ATTORNEY 1: That's okay.

Q. (By ATTORNEY 2) Was any part of the business run from your house?

A. Yes.

Q. What part of the business was run from your house?

A. Marketing x 2, PayPal, Vendor, our website G.B.G., and the website, answering emails and responding to emails.

Q. Did you ever meet with a vendor at your house?

A. Never at my house.

Q. Did you ever put your home address on any of

"My Business"'s documentation?

A. Yes.
Q. What?
A. PayPal. I know that Bank *** has it T has my home address.
Q. I'm not asking who has your home address. I'm asking –
A. Uses my home address.
Q. Okay. Anything else?
A. No.
Q. So what address, for example, is on your business license?
A. G's.
Q. Where did the bank statements get mailed?
A. Bank statements from Bank are only mailed to one person, and they go to G.
Q. What address was used on your tax returns?
A. G's.
Q. Were you ever present at meetings at G's house with vendors for "My Business"?
A. No.
Q. Are you aware of meetings that G had at her house for vendors with "My Business" even if you did not attend?
A. G never told me she was having meetings with vendors at her house that I am aware of or that I can recall.

> ***What I should have said was, "G should not have been having meetings without me". I should have either been made aware G was having them, or that G should not have had them without me being present.

My Crazy Deposition

Q. Where do you believe most of your clients came from? In other words, how did they come to learn of and use the services of "My Business"?

A. From the Internet.

Q. And what is the facts that you're aware of that support that belief?

A. I keep a log of the – on Marketing for the amount of hits that come through Marketing, and I can correlate the amount of hits through Marketing that click through to the amount of users that have signed onto Vender.

Q. How many customers do you understand Business to have?

A. I have no access to the website. I have no idea at this time how many customers we have.

Q. The last time you knew, what do you believe that number approximated?

A. I believe it was a little over twenty-seven hundred.

Q. And do you have any knowledge of where those customers each individually came from?

A. I would have no idea. We don't ask those questions from our customers.

Q. So when you say you believe most of them came from finding the company online, what's the basis of your saying that?

A. Because of the click throughs from Marketing on over to the amount of users that have logged in to Vendor on a daily basis.

Q. Are you aware of any data that correlates a click on Marketing to a *** taker?

A. Not to a test taker, no.

Q. So when you say customers, are you describing people who took tests?

A. Customers to me means people who logged into the site, not necessarily took a test, because not all customers – not all customers have taken tests.
Q. How many people have taken tests approximately the last time you knew?
A. I do not have that knowledge at this time.
Q. Not necessarily at this time. But the last time you were aware, what approximately was that number?
A. I do not have an estimated number.
Q. We know it's less than twenty-seven hundred, right?
A. Could you repeat that question?
Q. All I'm trying to find out is your best knowledge at whatever point in time it was of the number of people who had actually taken tests of materials that were on the "My Business" website.
A. I could not give you a specific number at this time.
Q. Again I'm not asking for a specific number. I'm asking for your best estimate.
A. I would have to refer back to the documents that were printed.
Q. Was it more than a hundred?
A. I cannot answer that question unless you're giving me a time frame.
Q. Ever. Total number of different people who took ***, total number.
A. Over a hundred, yes.
Q. Over two hundred?
A. Yes.
Q. Over a thousand? Not sure?
A. I don't want to estimate.
Q. Over five hundred?

My Crazy Deposition

A. I do not want to estimate a number.

Q. So your comfort level is two hundred to a thousand.

A. I do not want to estimate a number at this time.

Q. I understand. So is your comfort level -because you told me it's more than two hundred and you don't know if it's a thousand. So is your comfort level at least it's two hundred to a thousand?

A. I do not want to –

ATTORNEY 1: Objection.

THE WITNESS: – estimate that number.

ATTORNEY 1: Objection. The question is calling for speculation. She's already said she doesn't have the figures, and you keep pushing her more and more on that.

ATTORNEY 2: And I'm entitled to know something because obviously there's information in your head that's not in mine.

Q. Is it less than a hundred thousand?

A. Yes.

Q. We're going down. Are you comfortable saying, I know it's no more than that?

A. I do not want to estimate any numbers without being able to look at numbers.

Q. So then I have to ask my question, is it less than fifty thousand?

A. Yes.

Q. Is it less than ten thousand?

A. I don't know.

Q. It may be more than ten thousand?

A. I don't know. I don't have a figure without looking at my paperwork.

Q. Do you believe it is less than ten thousand?

B Kuffel

A. I do not want to estimate a number at this time.

Q. So it's somewhere between two hundred and ten thousand? That's the extent of your comfort level?

A. I do not want to estimate a number at this time.
ATTORNEY 1: Can I – Attorney 2, let me interrupt.
ATTORNEY 2: If you want to object -
ATTORNEY 1: No.
ATTORNEY 2: – make your objection.
ATTORNEY 1: Can we go off the record?
ATTORNEY 2: I'm not going off the record. We're asking questions. If you want to object, make an objection. You don't get to testify.
ATTORNEY 1: He's entitled to an estimate. What he's not entitled to is a guess. So if you have an estimate, you can give him your estimate, but don't guess, which there's a -

> ***There is a difference, but it is still held against you in court. I had not been monitoring this information, and did not have a true estimate for a 6 year period. I should have said that.

THE WITNESS: I don't want to guess.
ATTORNEY 1: Okay. But there's a difference. So if you do have an estimate, you need to give it to him.

THE WITNESS: I don't – I don't have an estimate in my mind at this time, and I do not want to guess.
ATTORNEY 1: I just want you to – okay.
That's fine.
THE WITNESS: I don't want to guess at numbers.

My Crazy Deposition

Q. (By ATTORNEY 2) Do you agree that the most important marketing sources were in fact in person in-services or presentations?

A. I do not agree with that.

Q. What do you disagree about that?

A. I believe there's more numbers marketing towards the Internet than going to a hospital where there may be 40 **** in a *******.

Q. How many in-services did "My Business" present?

ATTORNEY 1: Objection as to in-services.

ATTORNEY 2: I think your client knows what an in-service is.

ATTORNEY 1: Well, I don't.

ATTORNEY 2: It doesn't M.er. You're not asking questions.

ATTORNEY 1: That's fine. But I'm objecting. It's vague and ambiguous. · · · And if you can answer it, if you know, you can. But if you need clarification, that's fine.

THE WITNESS: I'm aware of two.

Q. (By ATTORNEY 2) Only two?

A. In-services, correct.

Q. Are you aware of other presentations which you or G made to **** staffs anywhere?

A. I am not aware of any other presentations that were made other than two, because the ***** when we looked into it were charging a vendor fee for us to go in and do presentations. So at the time that I knew of when those vendor fees were being asked to be charged, we were not paying those fees.

Q. What are the two in-services you're aware of?

A. The one at "Employer" R********, and I believe the second one was at "Employer" South Sacramento.

Q. In fact aren't you fully aware that G did many of them over the years?

A. I am not aware of –

ATTORNEY 1: Objection, vague and ambiguous as to many. Can we be clear, be clear on what you're asking here? This is argumentative –

Q. (By ATTORNEY 2) Isn't it correct that every time G did an in-service, there was a big spike in the number of tests taken right afterward?

A. I'm only aware –

ATTORNEY 1: Objection, vague and ambiguous as to big spike. How big?

ATTORNEY 2: Go ahead and answer.

ATTORNEY 1: Two people? Three people? Can you break it down. I mean you do the estimates with the other numbers. Maybe we can do it with this. Five people?

ATTORNEY 2: Go ahead and answer.

THE WITNESS: I'm sorry. Could we repeat the question exactly. I want to hear the question again. ATTORNEY 2: Go ahead. (Whereupon the last question "Isn't it correct that every time G did an in-service there was a big spike in the number of tests taken right afterward" was read back as requested.)

THE WITNESS: There was a spike in the amount of users that signed on. I never compared the amount of *** taken to the users that signed on. So I cannot verify the information, that particular information.

Q. (By ATTORNEY 2) Let's talk about a trip that you and G and your husbands took to Las Vegas.

My Crazy Deposition

A. Okay.
Q. You know what I'm talking about?
A. Yes, sir.
Q. Isn't it correct that the purpose of that trip was for you to make a presentation to a **** staff in Las Vegas?
A. No.
Q. Isn't it true that you would agree to make the presentation and G was going to have responsibility for the IT work while you made the presentation?

ATTORNEY 1: Objection, compound. Could you maybe not combine so many things in one question?

THE WITNESS: Could you clarify the question, please.

ATTORNEY 2: Could you repeat the question. (Whereupon the last question "Isn't it true that you would agree to make the presentation and G was going to have responsibility for the IT work while you made the presentation" was read back as requested.)

ATTORNEY 1: So my objection stands. There's two different activities -

ATTORNEY 2: You made your objection.

ATTORNEY 1: Fine. Can you break it down. She can't answer the question without saying yes or no or address each specific one. It's a compound question. Come on. This is absurd that you're being so dogged and not going back and correcting the question.

Q. (By ATTORNEY 2) Go ahead.
A. So that particular trip, there was actually two days involved in that trip. The first day, we mingled in a preconference where we both passed out business cards and talked to the people in that room. In the presentation the next day, we ended up both doing IT work and both did talk out loud

to the crowd. So we ended up doing both roles. We were not specific to one particular role.

Q. (By ATTORNEY 2) Wouldn't it be more accurate to say that when you were asked to speak, you froze and couldn't speak in public and had to sit down and let G give the presentation?

A. That's not true.

ATTORNEY 2: She answered the question.

ATTORNEY 1: I know she did.

Q. (By ATTORNEY 2) And isn't it true that G gave the presentation and her husband, C, did the IT work?

ATTORNEY 1: Objection. That's a compound question. Can we ask one question at a time, please. This isn't – this isn't rocket science. One question.

Q. (By ATTORNEY 2) Isn't that true?

ATTORNEY 1: One question. Can we do that?

THE WITNESS: Please repeat the question.

(Whereupon the question "And isn't it true that G gave the presentation and her husband,

C, did the IT work" was read back as requested.)

ATTORNEY 2: You already objected. You don't have to object again -

ATTORNEY 1: Okay.

ATTORNEY 2: – once it's been read.

ATTORNEY 1: You should correct the question though, and you know I'm right. Go ahead if you feel you can answer the question independently without -

ATTORNEY 2: You've made your objection.

ATTORNEY 1: All right.

THE WITNESS: So I would like to address the IT part of that question. And I was also involved in signing up the

My Crazy Deposition

customers for their free **s during that conference. That task was not only for C to do. We were all involved in signing up customers. Could we repeat the second –

Q. (By ATTORNEY 2) And did G do the presentation?
A. We both did the presentation.
Q. What did you present?
A. It's – I do not recall.
ATTORNEY 1: Objection, calls for a narrative –
Q. (By ATTORNEY 2) What did she –
A. I do not recall –
(Reporter interruption.)

> ***The reporter was getting very frustrated with the attorneys going back, and for talking all at once. This was the crazy part of this deposition.

(Discussion was held off the record.)
ATTORNEY 2: H, we were speaking at the same time, so we want to make it clear for the record.
Q. Do you have a recollection of what you presented at the conference in Las Vegas?
A. I do not recall.
Q. Do you have a recollection of what G presented?
A. I do not recall.
Q. Do you have a recollection of what her husband, C, did during the presentation?
ATTORNEY 1: Objection, calls for speculation.
THE WITNESS: I do not recall.
Q. (By ATTORNEY 2) Do you have a recollection of what your husband did?
A. My husband was not a part of signing up customers.
Q. He was off doing something else entirely?

A. Right.
Q. Wasn't C called in at the last minute only because you froze?
A. No.

ATTORNEY 1: Objection – you answered. So that's okay.

Q. (By ATTORNEY 2) As you sit here today, do you know the number of new enrollees that followed – that "My Business" obtained following that presentation in Las Vegas?
A. I do not recall.
Q. Do you have any knowledge of the number of people that you presented to in Las Vegas who ultimately took ****?
A. I do not recall.
Q. When someone signs up to take a ****, is there anything by which you track how they learned about "My Business"?
A. No.
Q. When someone comes to the website for the first time, is there any means by which you track how they learned of the website?
A. There is one way that I know of that you can track if the information is transferred in PayPal. Other than that, I do not know. I do not recall a different way at this moment without having access to the – and relooking at the different features.
Q. In this lawsuit you have complained about a trip that my client took to *****, right?
A. Yes, sir.
Q. Are you aware of the presentation she made to a ***** staff while she was in *****?
A. I do not know that she made a presentation to a ***** staff in *****.

My Crazy Deposition

Q. Are you aware of the number of new enrollees that signed up to take tests from "My Business" that were – that learned of "My Business" following that presentation in *****?

A. I do not have access to the account. I have no idea what information would be in that – in Vendor without being allowed to have my access back.

Q. In fact wasn't the month which followed her trip to ***** the single biggest month for **** taking that "My Business" has ever had?

A. I would have no idea, sir. I do not have access to the accounts.

> ****I should have said was G's vacation, not business trip.

ATTORNEY 1: Do you want to testify? I mean you can.

Q. (By ATTORNEY 2) How do you know that that trip G took to **** was not in the best interests of the company if you have no knowledge of the number of new enrollees who signed up for "My Business" tests after the trip to *****?

> ***I should have said was I saw no income increase from that trip, and the bank account never increased in funds. That could have been used more than one way in my favor. I did not think fast enough.

ATTORNEY 1: I would object. That's a compound question. Can you break it down, please. Can you just break it down.

ATTORNEY 2: Please answer the question.

You made your objection.

ATTORNEY 1: I know. I know, but why aren't you -

ATTORNEY 2: You objected.

Now answer the question.

ATTORNEY 1: I correct these things when people object to my question. It's simple.

THE WITNESS: Could you please reword of that question again – could you please repeat that question to me. (Whereupon the last question "How do you know that that trip she took to **** was not in the best interests of the company if you have no knowledge of the number of new enrollees who signed up for "My Business" tests after the trip to ****" was read back as requested.)

THE WITNESS: That trip was not a mutually agreed-upon trip to go to *****.

Q. (By ATTORNEY 2) And is that the only basis of your objection to the expenses of the trip?

A. I know that people at work were talking about her posting pictures and talking about her vacation on Marketing.

Q. And didn't those same people at work also talk about the presentation she made to the hospital in **** while she was there?

A. They did not.

Q. When is the last time you went through PayPal records?

A. I do not recall the exact date, but it would have been the first part of 2015.

Q. Let me sort of move forward in more database stuff and move like toward the end of 2014. So you had been working together for more than four years by then, right?

A. Yes, sir.

Q. In that four years, had you ever – you and G – ever had any significant disagreements?
ATTORNEY 1: Object –
THE WITNESS: We had -
ATTORNEY 1: Sorry. Go ahead.
THE WITNESS: We had a disagreement about her writing WTF on my ***** and the fact that she had edited it instead of C who was supposed to have been the one who was to be editing courses.
Q. (By ATTORNEY 2) Did you ever talk to C about what his beliefs, feelings, conclusions were after he read it?
ATTORNEY 1: Objection -
THE WITNESS: No.
ATTORNEY 1: – calls for hearsay testimony.
Q. (By ATTORNEY 2) Do you have any knowledge of what C thought of that course after he read it?
ATTORNEY 1: Objection, relevance.
THE WITNESS: C didn't read *****.
Q. (By ATTORNEY 2) How do you know he didn't?
A. G said she edited that course.
Q. Did she say that he didn't also edit it?
A. I do not recall her saying that C edited that course. The discussion was about her editing and writing WTF on that course.
Q. Is that the only disagreement you recall you and G having had through the end of 2014?

> **** There was a reason we did not have many disagreements and that was addressed in G's deposition. G's attorney was very careful not to bring that reason up.

A. That is not the only disagreement that we had through 2014.
Q. What other disagreements did you have?
ATTORNEY 1: Objection, calls for hearsay testimony. You can answer.
THE WITNESS: We had a disagreement over how my **** course was going to be posted to the site.
Q. (By ATTORNEY 2) Edited or posted?
A. Posted.
Q. Okay. What other disagreements?
A. The disagreement on her posting her course without allowing me to have the opportunity to view it per her agreement.
Q. What course was that?
A. I'm blank.
ATTORNEY 1: Is it on maybe this list?
THE WITNESS: No.
ATTORNEY 2: That's the ones she wrote.
THE WITNESS: ********.
Q. (By ATTORNEY 2) What year was that in?
A. That was 2015.
Q. Okay. We're only talking about things that arose before the end of 2014. Remember that.
A. Oh, I'm sorry.
Q. I asked you about disagreements that arose before the end of 2014. So are there any other than posting the ***** course and editing of the ****** course?
A. None that I can recall.
Q. As to the ***** course, was the only disagreement that you were wondering why G edited it?
A. And the fact she wrote WTF on my paper, correct.

Q. I'm not segregating those. That's fine.
A. Okay.
Q. And what was the disagreement about the posting of the **** course?
A. I don't know. I don't know what she was upset about me pre-loading that – preloading the site, which I had always done before, waiting for that course to be completed editing.
Q. I want to make sure I understand what that means. Did you put the course online –
A. No.
Q. – before it was edited?
A. No, no.
Q. So what did you do?
A. I hadn't actually done anything at that point, but she was upset about me preparing Vendor to receive that course.
Q. And your understanding of the scope of the disagreement is what you just said in your last answer, and that's it?
A. To the best of my knowledge, yes.
   What did you do about that disagreement?
   Did you talk it through?
A. We talked it through.
Q. And resolved it one way or the other?
A. We resolved it.
Q. About the ***** course, what did you do when you had a disagreement?
A. I had A re-edit that course.
Q. So talked it through and resolved it?
A. And resolved it.
Q. So you've only told me about two disagreements you had, and they were both talked through and resolved?

A. Those are the two that come to the best of my knowledge to mind.
Q. The ******* disagreement was somewhere in 2013?
A. Correct.
Q. When was the ***** posting disagreement?
A. Approximately January of 2015.
Q. So again I asked you about things –
A. I know, I'm sorry.
Q. – that happened as of the end of 2014, so that wasn't even in there either?
A. Correct.
Q. So realistically the only disagreement you had in four plus – almost four and a half years of working together was when she stepped forward and edited the ***** course?
A. To the best of my knowledge.

> ***I should have said yes because G was doing something we had not agreed to.

Q. And you talked it through and resolved it?
A. To the best of my knowledge, yes.
Q. By the end of 2014 – I do not want you to go into 2015 yet –
A. 2015.
Q. – but by the end of 2014, how much time were you spending on the business of "My Business" per week?
A. Ten to twenty hours.
Q. And for how long had that been true?
A. Approximately from going to days towards the end of 2011.
Q. So for at least three years, '12, '13 and '14?
A. Correct.

My Crazy Deposition

Q. Do you have any knowledge of how much time G was spending on the business of "My Business" in 2012 or '13 or '14?
A. I have no idea what she was spending on it.
Q. Do you have any reason to suspect it was any different than what you were?
A. I know that during the time that she had ****, there was less time spent on the company.
When was that?
A. I don't remember the exact date.
Q. By the end of 2014 – let me ask the summary question because I assume your answer is no – had any of your relationships with any of your vendors changed from what you last told me? Using the same companies to do the same work -
ATTORNEY 1: Objection, compound, vague and ambiguous.
Q. (By ATTORNEY 2) – right?
A. After J left, I went to G.B.G.. Those were the same vendors.
Q. So nothing changes over the next couple years, right?
A. Correct.
Q. Still using G.B.G., PayPal, Vendor?
Nothing different?
A. Correct.
Oh, I'm sorry. Could I retract that answer? I would like to change it. We did actually elicit C* in about mid 2014 to help raise our company back up once the site was changed. It dropped and C* was now to bring the company back up.
So C* with L was added in approximately 2014.

> ***This is difficult when you have more than 1 person with the same initial. This C* from here to the end of the deposition is a different person. We will no longer be talking about the editor.

Q. If you were to try to summarize what marketing efforts "My Business" did as of the end of 2014, how would you do that?
A. We – well, I did all the Computer work when it came to "Marketing".
Q. Social media?

> *** I am changing well known social media advertisers to "Marketing"

A. Social media.
ATTORNEY 1: Can you let her answer, Attorney 2? You can testify, or we can call you as a witness if you want. But just let her finish her thoughts.
ATTORNEY 2: You know, you inhibit her train of thought a whole lot more than mine. Why don't you just ignore him and answer my question, please.
ATTORNEY 1: It's interesting because you're the one interrupting her. I'm just asking you not to interrupt her. It's simple, okay? Let's go.
ATTORNEY 2: Why don't you read the question and then half of her answer back before her lawyer interrupted and let her finish her answer. (Whereupon the record "Answer: We – well, I did all the Computer work when it came to Marketing. Question: Social media? Answer: Social media" was read back as requested.)

My Crazy Deposition

(By ATTORNEY 2) And what other marketing?

A. And I worked with C* on – he had created a faceplate to our business which was routing hits towards our company as well.

Q. So let's talk about him for the moment.
How did you find C*?

A. When G. changed the website based on the *** stating that we had to do some updates to the site, G. created a situation where our website dropped from number one to number six the first day and number eight the second day. G and I had a conversation over it, and G realized that that had caused us harm, and she allowed me again to contact J who put us in contact with C*.

Q. Is it fair to say C*'s big pitch was maximizing search engine optimization?
ATTORNEY 1: Objection. What do you mean by big pitch? Vague and ambiguous. Can you please clarify your question, sir.

Q. (By ATTORNEY 2) Go ahead.

A. No, not all of C*'s helps to guide the company was just for the optimization part.

Q. Was that his primary pitch?
Objection, vague and ambiguous as to primary, and speculation. She doesn't know what his big pitch, what his speculation – or what his primary -
ATTORNEY 2: All you have to say is vague and ambiguous. That's an objection.
ATTORNEY 1: Do you know what -
ATTORNEY 2: The rest is testimony. Make your objection. I have no problem with your objections. Stop testifying for your client.

ATTORNEY 1: I'm not testifying.
ATTORNEY 2: You are. Everything you're saying -
ATTORNEY 1: You're doing more testifying than my client.
ATTORNEY 2: Excuse me. I'm talking now. Everything you say after vague and ambiguous is testimony. Make your objection, and stop talking. If she doesn't understand the question, she'll tell me.
ATTORNEY 1: Will you please stop raising your voice to me, Attorney 2. Really.
ATTORNEY 2: Why don't you –
ATTORNEY 1: You can have a -

> ***I wish the recorder had caught everything that was said in this exchange. I was not only shocked, but appalled by what was said. It really took me off guard. I would like to talk more about it, but since she did not catch what was said I cannot. There is no way something like this cannot affect a person in deposition. Looking back it must have not been going well for him to have said this.

ATTORNEY 2: – stop leaning all the way across the table. I'm sorry. Am I not supposed to be on the table?
ATTORNEY 2: Why don't you just make your objections -
ATTORNEY 1: Hold on.
ATTORNEY 2: – and stop talking.
ATTORNEY 1: Hold on. Excuse me. I'm not supposed to be here? Is that it? I'm not supposed to talk? I'm not

supposed to lean on the table? Is that it? You don't want me leaning on the table, Attorney 2?

***This exchange must have shocked the recorder as well, for her not to have caught all of it.

ATTORNEY 2: Half the time you're so close to me, I have to step back to get away from you.
ATTORNEY 1: Oh, my gosh.

***"Oh, my gosh" was right.

ATTORNEY 2: Just sit there and make your objections.
ATTORNEY 1: I'm sorry. I apologize to you. I hope I'm not making you uncomfortable.
ATTORNEY 2: You're making me very uncomfortable because you're about two feet from me, and you have been for the entire deposition.
ATTORNEY 1: Two feet? Really.
ATTORNEY 2: So make your objection.
ATTORNEY 1: This is a very small room, and we are at a table -

***To me this was an absolutely ridiculous accusation, and a ploy to make a bad situation even worse.

ATTORNEY 2: Make your objection.
– that's maybe three feet wide, and we're both sitting on the wide ends of it. So will -
ATTORNEY 2: What is your objection?
ATTORNEY 1: – you please stop raising your voice to me.

ATTORNEY 2: What is your objection?
ATTORNEY 1: I'm not making an objection.
ATTORNEY 2: Fine.
Q. So answer your question, ma'am.
ATTORNEY 1: What was the question?
THE WITNESS: Please, could you repeat the question.
ATTORNEY 2: Let me just repeat it.
Q. The question was, isn't it correct that

> ***Pay attention to any question that starts with "isn't it correct that"...

C^'s primary pitch was working to increase search engine optimization for "My Business"?
ATTORNEY 1: And my objection stands. Vague and ambiguous and speculative.
THE WITNESS: C is – his main pitch was not always optimization. He had the same thoughts behind the website that as you said all the web guys have had. His ideas on the coding was much different than M.'s.
Q. (By ATTORNEY 2) The goal was driving people to the website, right?

> *** Attorney 2 is answering for me again. In court he would say "You agreed". No I did not, and would not have agreed, this line was very frustrating.

ATTORNEY 1: Objection. You're testifying. Can you just let her answer her questions. If that was a question, then ask her a question. But stop making these assertions, summarizing what she said.

My Crazy Deposition

ATTORNEY 2: What is your objection?

ATTORNEY 1: You're testifying. You're the attorney. You're not supposed to be testifying. You're supposed to be asking questions, not making assertions.

ATTORNEY 2: What is your objection?

ATTORNEY 1: You're testifying. The objection -

ATTORNEY 2: Fine. Then you made it.

Answer the question, please.

ATTORNEY 1: I was talking still, but fine.

THE WITNESS: Could you please clarify that question.

ATTORNEY 2: Could you repeat the question, please, *****.

THE WITNESS: I mean could you please clarify the question.

ATTORNEY 2: Let's hear the question. (Whereupon the last question "The goal was driving people to the website, right" was read back as requested.)

Q. (By ATTORNEY 2) Isn't that correct?

You've made your objection.

THE WITNESS: Yes.

> *** I should not have answered; I should have asked him to repeat the question because of the 2nd "isn't that correct". He could have put that to anything. I was still shocked at the exchange that had just taken place. I should have asked for a break.

ATTORNEY 1: I have another objection, but all right. Go ahead.

ATTORNEY 2: Thank you.

Q. Do you perceive that anything C*. did helped the business of "My Business"?
A. Yes.
Q. How?
A. He increased the amount of traffic that was going to the business.
Q. How do you know?
A. The amount of traffic had dropped when M. made the changes to the site, and you could correlate that with the amount of users that were signing up for the site.
Q. How do you know that?
A. I was tracking that in a log.
Q. How do you know there's a relationship between anything C* did and **** actually taken?
A. I don't know that.
Q. In fact didn't you check and conclude that there was no relationship between C*'s work and the number of **** taken?
A. I'm sorry, could you please repeat that question.
Q. Sure. Didn't you and G discuss what C* had done for you and conclude that there was no gain in tests taken by anything he wanted to do for you?
A. No.
ATTORNEY 1: Objection –
Q. (By ATTORNEY 2) C* is a big fan of social media, right?
ATTORNEY 1: Objection, vague and ambiguous as to what is meant by big fan of social media, and calls for speculation on the part of Mr., as to what he's a big fan of. She doesn't have personal knowledge. She can't testify as to what he's a big fan of or not. Why are you asking her -
ATTORNEY 2: You've made your objection.

ATTORNEY 1: Okay. I've made it.

ATTORNEY 2: Now answer the question, please.

ATTORNEY 1: If you can. If you can speak as to something -

ATTORNEY 2: You made your objection.

ATTORNEY 1: – that you don't have personal knowledge of, answer the question if you can.

THE WITNESS: I do not know what C*'s

personal thoughts are.

Q. (By ATTORNEY 2) Didn't he make it clear in his conversations with you that he was a big fan of Marketing and Marketing?

ATTORNEY 1: Objection, calls for hearsay.

Actually your question was hearsay.

THE WITNESS: C* made it clear that Marketing and Marketing – all based on information that he could show – would always help a business grow.

Q. (By ATTORNEY 2) Are you personally aware of what it costs to maintain a commercial Marketing account?

ATTORNEY 1: Objection, speculation.

THE WITNESS: Could you please clarify by what you mean by commercial.

Q. (By ATTORNEY 2) Well, you could have one personally for yourself –

A. Correct.

Q. – which doesn't cost anything to put online?

A. Uh-huh.

Q. Is a commercial Marketing account free?

A. No.

Q. So are you aware what it costs to operate or to have a commercial Marketing account?

A. Yes.

How are you billed?

A. Monthly.

ATTORNEY 1: Objection, billed for what?

> ***He was right, in my mind I thought I knew what he was asking; I could have just answered for anything.

Q. (By ATTORNEY 2) What are you charged for?
A. Could I change – I would like to correct my answer.

> *** I realized what I had said, and tried to correct it.

ATTORNEY 1: Objection, vague and ambiguous. How are you billed for what?
Q. (By ATTORNEY 2) Go ahead.
ATTORNEY 1: Commercial? Personal? What? Car rental?
Q. (By ATTORNEY 2) Go ahead, H. You started to answer. You said monthly, and then you said you wanted to change it.
A. Marketing actually will charge more than once a month. Depends on how much you're setting up for the amount that you wish to spend for bids to receive clicks.
Q. Do you agree that there is some charge Marketing imposes based on the number of likes and comments you get?
A. No.
Q. So every time someone clicks the like button, you get a fee, right?
A. Our particular site received it on bids.
So are you disagreeing with what I just said?
You don't think that was the case?
A. The way our site was set up, it was a bidding process. There was not necessarily a cost per click but a cost for that ad.
Q. I'm sorry, I don't know what you mean by bid. Who's bidding for what?
A. Companies are bidding for the ability to place an ad somewhere on Marketing.

Q. So let me ask you this way.
Was "My Business" charged a fee for every like on Marketing?
A. No.
ATTORNEY 1: Objection, asked and answered.
Q. (By ATTORNEY 2) Was Marketing– I'm sorry.
Was "My Business" charged a fee for every comment on Marketing?
A. No.
Q. Are you absolutely positive of that?
A. For a comment, no.
Q. How about for a like?
I'm sorry, you said no, meaning, no, you're not positive? You're not sure?
A. No, we are not charged for a like. We are charged for a bid. I'm not asking about bids. I used the word "like" and "comment."
Do you know what like and comment are on Marketing?
A. Yes, sir.
Q. You can click a box that's a like; you can click a box that's a comment?
A. Yes.
Q. When you click a box and it's a like, did Marketing charge you?
A. No.
Q. When someone clicked a box and it was a comment, did Marketing charge you?
A. No.
Q. What was the average monthly expense that "My Business" was paying Marketing?
ATTORNEY 1: Objection. It calls for speculation. THE WITNESS: It varied.

Q. (By ATTORNEY 2) From what to what?
A. We were spending approximately a dollar eighty a day. There were certain days when the bid was upped a little bit for holidays or special events to try to win the bids during that time frame.
Q. So are you saying your Marketing was costing you about fifty bucks a month?
ATTORNEY 1: Objection, mischaracterizing her prior comment.
ATTORNEY 2: A dollar eighty a day times 30. I think you can figure that out.
ATTORNEY 1: I'm sure, but that's not what she said.
Q. (By ATTORNEY 2) What was your monthly expense to Marketing?
A. It varied, but approximately a dollar eighty a day. That was the minimum amount that you could post to keep your Marketing account opened.
Q. So was your bill from Marketing approximately 54 dollars a month?
A. Approximately.
Q. For how long? In other words, for how many months was that the average?
A. From 2012 to the time that I was – G stopped the advertising in February of 2015.
Q. Are you aware of how many Marketing followers "My Business" had at any point in time?
A. I am.
Q. And when is the last time you're aware of that number?
A. February of 2015.
Q. And what was the number?
A. I had gotten it up to two thousand.

Q. And do you perceive two thousand is a significant number?

A. That was the goal to get it up to to be able to turn it over to C* to put it into the business aspect. I had to hit a certain number before it actually became a viable.

Q. And did Marketing cost "My Business" anything?

A. No.

Q. Marketing was always free?

A. Yes.

Q. Did you and G discuss the reasonableness of spending money for Marketing?

A. Yes.

Q. Did you and G discuss the reasonableness of paying C* what he asked you to pay him to increase your web presence?

ATTORNEY 1: Objection, assumes facts not present and also calls for potential hearsay testimony.

THE WITNESS: G and I agreed that we would pay the amount of money for C* to optimize the site.

Q. (By ATTORNEY 2) What does that mean?

A. We agreed to pay the ****** dollars a month.

Q. ***** dollars a month or ***** dollars?

A. C* charged ***** dollars a month, and we agreed to try it for six months.

Q. And what six months were those?

A. I don't remember – I don't recall the exact month we started because there were certain things that had to happen before that started. Approximately October of 2014.

Q. Do you agree that G was opposed to paying that sum, but you wanted to do it, and she said, fine, let's do it?

ATTORNEY 1: Objection, relevance.

THE WITNESS: She knew there was a problem with the website, and she agreed to give it a try.

Q. (By ATTORNEY 2) That's not what I asked.

A. I don't recall G opposing it. I remember G agreeing to try it.

Q. Do you perceive that that was a coGromise between business owners because you wanted to do something, and she didn't, and she said, let's do it?

A. I don't recall G opposing trying this process, because what was going on wasn't working.

Q. And did you later conclude that his expenses weren't generating enough money to pay for what he was charging you?

A. No, I did not conclude that.

Q. Did you discuss with G whether she believed that?

ATTORNEY 1: Objection, calls for hearsay testimony and – yeah.

THE WITNESS: At the time the six months was up, I was already locked out of the site. We didn't have a discussion around that.

Q. (By ATTORNEY 2) Isn't it true that C* gave you a separate proposal where he wanted to charge you a *** dollars a month?

After you hired him to do the *** hundred a month, didn't he give you a proposal to spend a *** dollars a month?

A. He didn't change the *** hundred dollars a month. There was a proposal that if we chose to buG the package up, we could pay the *** dollars a month.

Q. And in fact he wanted *** dollars down plus a *** a month, didn't he?

A. I do not recall that.

Q. Do you recall discussing with G at that time there was no money to pay him *** dollars down and a *** dollars a month?
A. We were not agreeing -
ATTORNEY 1: Object -
THE WITNESS: – to pay *** dollars a month and a *** – we never agreed to that. That was not an option.
Q. (By ATTORNEY 2) Do you know as you sit here today what you earned from "My Business" on an annual basis?
A. I could not recall the exact figures off the top of my head, but I do have those figures written down.
Q. In 2010 you personally – in other words, your share – you lost **** dollars, right?
A. That's what the K-1 reflects.
Q. And in 2011, you lost *** dollars, right?
A. I don't recall the exact figures in –
Q. Does that sound approximate, though, a small loss?
A. I don't recall that we lost. I don't remember.
I don't recall.
Q. And in 2012, you made a *** dollars?
A. I don't recall the exact figures.
Q. Does that sound approximately correct even though you don't know the exact number?
A. I would have to look at my documentation to verify those figures.
Q. I understand, but I'm entitled to test your recollection.
A. Uh-huh.
Q. So does that sound approximately correct to you?
A. Could you repeat that.
Q. A **** 2012?
A. I thought it was more than that.

My Crazy Deposition

Q. What did you believe – what would you have estimated if I hadn't given you the number?
A. Repeat the year, please.
Q. 2012.
A. We're basing these figures off the K-1?
Q. Yes.
A. That's probably close in 2012.
Q. And what would you remember your 2013 K-1 to reflect?
A. I don't recall the exact numbers.
Q. **** sound right?
A. Pretty close.
Q. And how about 2014, do you remember that?
A. No, I don't recall the exact figures.
Q. What's your estimate?
A. It was more than the previous year, but I don't recall.
Q. In fact wasn't it less? You made less in 2014 than '13?
A. I don't recall making less.
Q. You made **** in 2014.
   Does that sound right?
A. What was 2013?
Q. ****.
A. 2014 – 2014, we did do worse after M. made the changes to the site, that is correct.
Q. So in five years of doing business, you had made a grand total of **** dollars, correct? Five years, **** dollars? That's just the sum of those five numbers I've given you.

> ***Where attorney 2 came up with this made up number I have no idea, but this was also the number he used in court. This number was his

words not mine. That was part of the argument, the amounts per year were not correct.

A. You said **** thousand, **** hundred, **** thousand –
Q. But you lost the **** dollars the first year.
A. I don't – I understand what you're saying, but I disagree on the first year because that was just a start-up business.
Q. And you knew that? You had that information in mind when you were talking to C* in 2014 about what he would charge you, right?
A. Yes.
Q. So he was proposing a **** dollar flat fee and a **** dollars a month for a business that had made *** dollars in five years?

ATTORNEY 1: Objection, compound question, objection. It's also – you're also calling for hearsay testimony of Mr. .. So if you maybe could break down the question, that would be more helpful rather than the string of verbiage before it.

THE WITNESS: Could you please clarify the question.

> ***Attorney 2 took this going back and forth over numbers he made up and he presented those figures in court. These figures he kept quoting were not correct for any of the amounts the business had earned in any one year. I should not have fell into this line of questions. The 2014 and the 2015 K1's were not correct, and one of the issues that I was fighting in court.

My Crazy Deposition

Q. (By ATTORNEY 2) All I'm asking you, is it correct that you knew all that? You had all those numbers available to you when you were talking to C* .?
A. So now I'm not understanding the question. The question has changed.
Q. You've told me what your gross profits or gross losses were on an annual basis. And all I'm clarifying is, you knew that. You know it today, but you knew it then when you were talking to C* ., right?

> ***He was he going to use this against me in court.

ATTORNEY 1: Objection. That's a compound question.
ATTORNEY 2: It's a yes or no question.
ATTORNEY 1: You've said a half dozen things

in there.

>ATTORNEY 2: It's a yes or no question.
>
>ATTORNEY 1: She can't answer yes to one without answering yes to all those other points, and it's a compound question. She's entitled to not have to answer a question like that. Could you please rephrase the question.
>
>THE WITNESS: Our agreement with C*. was to pay **** hundred dollars a month.

Q. (By ATTORNEY 2) That's not what I'm asking you, okay? What I'm asking you, notwithstanding what he's saying, is literally a very simple yes or no question. What I'm asking you is, did you have the knowledge in your head of your prior years' earnings when you were talking to C*. about what he was suggesting to charge you?

>ATTORNEY 1: Objection, calls for hearsay testimony, and also it's kind of – well, all right.
>
>THE WITNESS: Could you clarify the amount that you're talking about that C*. was –

> ***He was throwing out two different amounts, and I wanted to make sure what amount he was asking about.

Q. (By ATTORNEY 2) In 2014, did you know what you'd earned in 2010?

A. I'm asking about the question that you asked me to clarify the amount that C*. was asking us to pay.

Q. That's not pertinent to the question that is pending before you. Do you know what you made in 2010? You just told me; so you know it, right?

> ***I made a huge mistake here, I should not have answered with a yes. He used his figures and this yes to use his made up number for income in court.

A. Yes.
Q. And did you know it in 2014?
A. Yes.
Q. And in 2011, you knew what you made?
A. Yes.
Q. And did you have that knowledge in 2014?
A. Yes.
Q. And in 2012, you know what you made?
A. Yes.
Q. And did you have that in 2014?
A. Yes.
Q. And in 2013, you know what you made?
A. Yes.
Q. And did you have that in late 2014 when you were talking to C* .?
A. Yes.
Q. Okay. So you already knew all those numbers when you were talking to C*. That's all I'm asking.
A. Yes.
Q. Okay. Thank you. And you're telling me as I understand it that you do not have a recollection of G saying you couldn't afford C* .; is that correct?
ATTORNEY 1: Objection, calls for hearsay testimony.
THE WITNESS: No, I do not remember G saying when we agreed to the **** hundred dollars that we could not afford him.

ATTORNEY 2: Let's go off the record for a minute.
(Lunch recess taken from 12:15 p.m. to 1:00 p.m.)

> *** I needed this break to get out of this room. I am not a claustrophobic person, but the room seem to be getting smaller.

Q. (By ATTORNEY 2) Ms., I want to move forward. I was trying to focus prior to the end of 2014, and now I want to move into 2015, okay?

> ***I did not realize we were focusing on the end of 2014, it seemed to me he was still jumping around with dates.

A. Okay.
Q. So let's start with the simplest. I'll let you describe for me what you perceive to be the source of your disagreement with G.
A. G posted a course that had *** **** as well as grammerical errors. And I was not allowed to view that course before that happened.
ATTORNEY 2: Excuse me just for a second. I left a pad on my desk that I keep my notes on.
(Brief recess taken.)

ATTORNEY 2: Could you read what she said?
(Whereupon the last answer "G posted a course that had **** **** as well as grammerical errors. And I was not allowed to view that course before that happened" was read back as requested.)

Q. (By ATTORNEY 2) What were the materials that you believed to be *****?
A. There were *** ***** images, images that ******, and there were several misspelled words, spacing issues, pages weren't numbered. A lot of different types of grammerical misspellings in there.
Q. Okay. And your belief that they were ***** ***** was because it said that on the ***** somewhere?

> *** I must not have heard the question correctly or was thinking about a past question. Looking back these types of answers really surprise me when I see how I must have been so distracted to give an answer to a completely different question. It is so important to stay focused, a wrong answer can be so detrimental in court.

A. No. G when she responded to me in her text said she was allowed to use *** percent ***** material and that her attorneys – her attorney friends told her she could do that.
Q. You disagreed –
A. I did.
Q. – right?
What is the basis of your disagreement?
ATTORNEY 1: Objection, calls for -potentially calls for attorney/client privileged communication. But if you can answer without disclosing attorney/client information, by all means. So if it's only attorney/client communication, then you don't want to necessarily disclose that. I mean it's up to you, but I would advise you not to.

Q. (By ATTORNEY 2) In other words, you need to answer my question. But in answering the question, you don't need to disclose something that you only know because a lawyer told you, okay. So if that's the answer, then tell me "because a lawyer told me," and I won't ask you what the lawyer told you.
ATTORNEY 1: But any other information you acquired from other sources would be available for his question.
THE WITNESS: Okay. So I did do some research on the Internet. ***********************

Q. (By ATTORNEY 2) And that was the basis of your determining that G was wrong –
A. No.
Q. – what you researched, yourself?
A. I did contact an attorney also to verify that.
Q. What attorney did you contact, without telling me what you and he or she discussed? ATTORNEY 1: You can tell him.
THE WITNESS: Attorney A.
Q. (By ATTORNEY 2) So when you recognized that you had this disagreement because you didn't think that G should have posted it, what did you do?
A. Could you please repeat that question.
Q. Sure. What was your first step after you realized G did something that you didn't think she should have done?
A. Well, when I went on Vendor and saw that the ***** was activated, at that point I didn't know whether or not she meant to ****** that course, so I ******* it. And then I had – was forwarding G all the corrections that I felt needed to be done to that course and that we needed to fix those

My Crazy Deposition

before the course was actually ****** to the public. And I had – that's what I did in the beginning.

***I realized I was going to add too much, and decided I should stop. This is why this is such a choppy answer.

Q. So step number one is you ***** the course; step number two is you forwarded proposed corrections to G?
A. Step number one is that I actually completed editing the – looking at the ***** and writing out the problems that I felt were the issues, emailed that. And then when I went onto Vendor and saw that it was *****, I didn't – I ***** it at that time.
Q. So you've added a third step in there –
A. I'm sorry.
Q. – edit, *******, forward to G.
   It sounds like you **** before you ******?
A. I **** before I *********.
Q. But you ******* before you forwarded to G?
A. No, I did the ***** and then forwarding of the email and then the *******.
Q. And what was G's response?
A. She asked me, did I ***** the course. I said yes. G – I don't recall the specifics of the conversation, but the end result was G told me, do not ****** the ***** again.
Q. And she ***** it?
A. And she ******* it.
Q. And then what did you do?
A. I placed a call to Attorney A.
Q. And then after that call, what did you do next?
A. I didn't actually connect with him until –

ATTORNEY 1: Objection.

Q. (By ATTORNEY 2) Well, I don't care what you and he discussed.

ATTORNEY 1: Yeah.

THE WITNESS: Oh.

> ***I continually forgot about the attorney client privilege. I did not have anything to hide, but I should have used it when appropriate. That may have forced him to move on or reword some of his questions.

Q. (By ATTORNEY 2) What did you guys do about the course or the business?

A. I'm sorry. I informed her that due to attorney consultation, the ******** should be removed from the ***** and that I deactivated the course until we could correct those ********.

Q. So you ******* a second time?

> ***This became very important in court. G and attorney 2 claimed something based on this information from this line of questions. I did not realize how the smallest of answers can be turned against you. He used this question to create a different question to use against me in court.

A. Correct.

Q. And then what happens?

A. We attempted to meet, and that was not able to happen. And G asked me to call her on Friday over lunch, and I did.
Q. So you've described that you ****** it a second time. Did G ***** it, or did it stay *****?
ATTORNEY 1: Objection, compound.
THE WITNESS: It was ***** at some time, at some point.
Q. (By ATTORNEY 2) How long was it between your first **** and G's *****?
A. I estimate – because I don't know the times that she actually ****** it –
Q. That's fine.
A. – is probably 12 hours.
Q. And how long was it between that and your ****** deactivation?
A. Four days before – no, I'm sorry.
Probably five days because I talked –

> ***He was not liking my answer, and I should have insisted to complete it. If he did not like the way the answer was going he would just interrupt.

Q. Okay. And how long is it before she **** it a second time?
A. She had as of Friday changed the passwords and effectively locking me out of the website. And it was ****** as far as I know after she deactivated the password –
Q. Well, your saying it happened on a Friday doesn't help us because we haven't put days of the week to any of the conversations.
A. I'm sorry. We're talking –

Q. Let me finish.
Approximately how many days is it between your second ****** and her second ******?

A. I don't know the –
ATTORNEY 1: Objection because it calls for her to speculate as to when G ****** it. But to the best of your ability, answer.
THE WITNESS: I don't know when she ****** it.

Q. (By ATTORNEY 2) Hours or days?

A. I don't know. I was locked out of the account.
I have no idea when she ****** it.

Q. And what other steps do you understand G to have taken in response to this ***** ****** by you?

A. Could you please clarify that question.

Q. Sure. You have said, she locked me out. You've used that phrase a couple times. What does that mean? What does –

A. She changed the –

Q. Hang on. What do you understand she did? Tell me all the things that you think she did.

A. She changed the passwords to Vendor and to our website G.B.G., effectively locking me out of those two sites.

Q. Anything else?

A. Could you please repeat the question.

Q. Sure. I'm just asking, is there anything else you are asserting that she did which you believe to have been improper?

A. She ****** the course that still had grammerical errors.

Q. Anything else?

A. Not that I can think of at this moment.

Q. As to G.B.G., you said she changed the password. Isn't it correct that G changed G's password?

A. It was the company's password.

My Crazy Deposition

Q. You had the ability to log on with your own password if you had wanted to, didn't you?

A. Not to G.B.G.. I never had my own individual password.

Q. With Vendor, isn't it correct that all G changed was G's password?

A. She changed the S.U. password that was connected to the business. That's the password that I used to get in and out of the Vendor for the company.

Q. But there was nothing that stopped you from having your own password if you had wanted, right?

A. The password that I was using was to my personal account that I logged in to take ***** as a customer which allowed me only access to pay for and take an exam in order to have credit for my ******.

Q. But there was nothing that stopped you from having your own password to anything that belonged to "My Business"?

A. All businesses only had one password that was linked to a company. They did not have the ability or did not have the option in order for each individual person to have their own password to get in and out of the business portion of those of our company.

Q. How do you know that?

A. I asked.

Q. Who did you ask?

A. J* and – and M. told me that I could not have my own.

Q. Who is M.?

A. M. from G.B.G., M.

Q. M? And he said you can't have your own password?

A. He said the companies only have one password.

Q. And J*, what was his response?

A. It's a S.U., and only one S.U. per company.

Q. So after you learned that G did these things you described, what did you do?
A. We sought mediation to see if we could resolve our differences.
Q. Well, there were things that happened before that.
ATTORNEY 1: Objection. You're assuming facts not in evidence. You want to testify here?
Q. (By ATTORNEY 2) What's the first thing you –
A. Oh, I did email G and asked her to please reinstate my access to the accounts.
Q. Anything else?
A. Not that I can recall at the moment.
Q. Do you agree that you told her that you did not want to be partners any longer?
A. I never said that.
Q. Never ever?
A. I did not say –
ATTORNEY 1: Asked and answered.
THE WITNESS: – in specific words that I did not want to be partners with her. I never said those words to her.
Q. (By ATTORNEY 2) Did you ever tell anyone other than conversations with your lawyers that you didn't want to be partners with G?
A. I never used the terms I did not want to be partners with G.
Q. Did you use words to that effect?
A. No.
Q. Did you at any point tell her that you wanted to end your partnership?
A. I never used the words that I wanted to end -that I wanted to end our partnership.

My Crazy Deposition

Q. Again did you use words to that effect?
A. No.
Q. What do you understand your partnership agreement to have required when you came to some disagreement like you did in this case?
ATTORNEY 1: I'm sorry, could you ask -could you repeat the question for me. Sorry. (Whereupon the last question "What do you understand your partnership agreement to have required when you came to some disagreement like you did in this case" was read back as requested.)
ATTORNEY 2: You have to answer the question. You can't keep looking at him every time I ask a question.

> ***This was funny to me because my attorney had instructed me to look at him, and give him time to object.

ATTORNEY 1: I think the best – I'm going to object to that as calling for a legal conclusion. ATTORNEY 2: Okay. You made your objection.
Q. Answer the question now, please.
A. We tried to work it out, and it wasn't ever specifically addressed how we would have to work out an issue between the two of us.
Q. Okay. I think you may have answered part of that because you said we tried to work it out, and I'm not asking what you did.
I'm asking for your understanding, no legal conclusion, nothing else, your subjective understanding of it – might be right, might be wrong – but what was your understanding of what your partnership agreement required you to do when you came to an impasse?

ATTORNEY 1: I'm objecting as – again it calls for a legal conclusion.

ATTORNEY 2: Fine. You've made your objection.

Q. Now answer the question.

A. At this time I don't recall how our partnership addressed an iGasse.

Q. Did you think about it back in 2015?

A. I don't know that I looked at the contract to try to – I looked at the contract, and it didn't really address how we would resolve an impasse.

Q. Did you have any understanding at the time of what California law would have required?

ATTORNEY 1: Objection. Again you're asking her to speculate in areas that only an expert would be qualified to testify as to her – someone knowledgeable in the law. She's not required to understand -

ATTORNEY 2: Again I'm not asking her that at all.

ATTORNEY 1: She's not required to know what the law is or anything to that effect.

(By ATTORNEY 2) Again he's trying to get you to answer questions different than I am. I'm not asking what the law is. I'm asking your understanding. You may have no understanding. But I'm asking you, did you have any understanding of what the law would have provided separate and apart from your partnership agreement?

A. No, I did not. That's why I sought out legal counsel.

Q. Subsequent to February of 2015, did you **** any further **** for "My Business"?

A. No.

Q. Did you solicit any further customers for "My Business"?
A. No.
Q. Did you provide any in-services for the business?
A. No.
Q. Meet with any of its vendors?
A. I did have contact with the vendors.
Q. With whom?
A. J*. M. made it clear that he wasn't going to help me in any way so I didn't contact, other than to again request us be onto the site. I didn't have any further contact with J*.
Did you have any conversations with J* or M other than what you've already told me?
ATTORNEY 1: Objection, calls for hearsay testimony.
THE WITNESS: Yes.
Q. (By ATTORNEY 2) What conversations did you have – with which of them did you have conversations you haven't already told me about?
A. I called J* to make sure that the bills were being paid.
Q. Anything else other than that you ever discussed with him?
A. I called him back again to make sure the consecutive year that our material was not lost.
Q. Have you now told me of all the conversations you've had with J*?
ATTORNEY 1: Objection, potentially calls for -
THE WITNESS: I cannot -
ATTORNEY 1: Potentially calls for hearsay testimony.
THE WITNESS: I cannot recall at this moment.
Q. (By ATTORNEY 2) Have you told me about all the conversations you've had with M?
A. Yes. That I am aware of, yes.

After February of 2015, did you ever meet with the accountant who was doing the tax returns for "My Business"?

A. We don't have an accountant.

Q. An accountant has prepared your tax returns, hasn't he?

A. I don't know that he's an accountant. I know that he's a tax preparer. Yes, I have contacted V multiple times about the tax return.

Q. What year's tax return, and when did you talk to him?

A. 2014. I cannot remember the specific dates, but I talked to him several times prior to the tax return being filed.

Q. Sometime in the spring of 2015 about the 2014 returns?

A. I believe it was before March 15th.

Q. And didn't V ask you to identify for him any coGlaints you have about the tax return?

ATTORNEY 1: Objection, calls for hearsay testimony of Mr. V, and also potentially a narrative. THE WITNESS: I'm sorry, could you repeat the question.

(By ATTORNEY 2) Sure. I'm just asking you, when did you – you and V talked in the spring. What did you talk about?

A. I told him that the information that was on the tax return was incorrect.

Q. You disagreed with it, right?

A. I did.

Q. And he sent you a draft of the return he was going to file, right?

A. Yes.

Q. And he told you, if you have any objections, tell me, right?
ATTORNEY 1: Objection.

THE WITNESS: He did, and I did object multiple times with V about filing that tax return.

Q. (By ATTORNEY 2) In fact didn't you completely ignore his efforts to communicate with you?

A. I did not –

ATTORNEY 1: Objection.

THE WITNESS: – ignore any efforts from V.

Q. (By ATTORNEY 2) And didn't he eventually file the tax returns because you never responded to his requests that you voice your objections?

ATTORNEY 1: Objection, again calls for hearsay testimony, and also it's argumentative and assuming facts not in – not on the record. So you can go ahead and answer if you'd like.

THE WITNESS: I did voice my concerns to V and asked him not to file that tax return, and he said G was pushing him to do it. And so he said, "I have to file it anyway because G says I have to file the tax return."

Q. (By ATTORNEY 2) Wasn't his last communication to you one that said, "I haven't heard from you so I'm going to go ahead and file the tax returns"?

ATTORNEY 1: Objection, are you – calls for hearsay testimony, and also I feel like you're testifying here, Attorney 2. But go ahead and answer.

THE WITNESS: The communication that I got – I communicated to V that I needed to talk to my attorney, and that as soon as I was able to contact my attorney, I would get back to him. And when I got back to him on that communication, I specifically told him that I had not heard from the attorney and I was waiting for their communication. So he did hear back from me even though that was his last communication.

Q. (By ATTORNEY 2) After February of 2015, did you undertake any efforts to expand the business of "My Business"?

A. No.

Q. Did you make any –

A. I had no access to "My Business". I was locked out of everything. There was no way for me to expand anything.

Q. I understand that's your position. We're leaving that as a given for the moment. I don't necessarily agree with it, but I understand that's your position. Did you undertake any efforts to increase the number of customers or clients of "My Business"?

A. I had no access to the accounts. I had no way of really –

Q. So is the answer no?

A. The answer is no, but I'm not finished with my answer. The answer is no because I was not able to access anything to be able to even advertise to any of our clients or customers that we already had, and no ability to do it through any other avenue. I had no access to anything.

Q. The Marketing account was still active, wasn't it?

A. No. When she stopped paying the bill, they shut the Marketing part of it down.

Q. Isn't it still active today?

A. You can go to it, but it's not active on the business aspect of that part of the company.

Q. And is the Marketing account still active?

A. I don't know. I haven't been to the Marketing account.

Q. So no one stopped you from going to it, right?

A. No one stopped me; however, Marketing does not allow you to do any kind of communication on that site when the bill is not paid.

Q. Did you send out any other marketing brochures after February of 2015?

A. No.

Q. Did you undertake any efforts whatsoever to promote the business of "My Business"?

A. No.

Q. As of February of 2015, did you still want to have an interest in "My Business"?

A. Yes.

Q. So you certainly had an effort – I'm sorry.
You certainly had an incentive to continue its operations?

A. Yes.

Q. You certainly had an effort to see the business be successful?

A. I wanted the –
ATTORNEY 1: Objection as to –

Q. (By ATTORNEY 2) You had an incentive to see the business thrive and continue to grow?

A. I did want the business to continue to thrive and grow. However, I had no way of getting into the business to be able to make that happen. I couldn't respond to emails. There's no way I could actually – if new customers came in, there was no way for me to be able to have any type of communication or any type of access to them to even be able to follow through. There was no ability for me to be able to follow through for any new customers that came into that company. So it would seem to me that would be difficult to tell somebody to come to the business and then not be able to communicate with that person if I'm locked out.

Q. At any point after February of 2015, did you atteGt to sell the business to a third party?

A. Never.

Q. Why not?

A. That's not what our agreement says.

Q. Well, without regard to what the agreement says, why can't you make that effort?

Objection. She just answered the question. Sorry, I think you went a different direction in your follow-up. So I apologize. Go ahead.

THE WITNESS: I'm sorry?

Q. (By ATTORNEY 2) The question is simply, why?

A. Why didn't I try to sell the business?

Q. Yes.

A. Because I was still trying to resolve the business prior to ever moving on. I can't sell the business out from underneath G. That would be I feel against my fiduciary duty since we were still partners to try to sell the business out from underneath her. I would never do that.

Q. Did you ever say to G, why don't we sell the business?

A. No.

Q. Why not?

A. I felt we still hadn't resolved the issues between us on possibly either buying it or selling it between the two of us.

Q. Did you ever make an offer to buy the business from G?

ATTORNEY 1: Objection, calls for – well, I withdraw that.

THE WITNESS: No.

My Crazy Deposition

Q. (By ATTORNEY 2) Why not?
A. Because G made the offer, and according to our partnership agreement, she's also supposed to make an offer for me to buy the business. And since that had never been really addressed through this process, I was still trying to resolve it as we initially had started it.
Q. Let me back up a little bit because I'm not sure you answered the question. I asked you if you ever made an effort to buy the business from G, and you said no. And I'm asking you, why not?
A. Because in the partnership agreement when she makes an offer to purchase the company, she's also supposed to make an offer for me to be able to buy the business. And in that contract that she kept sending me, that was never addressed, and I was hoping we could work through that process.
Q. You're answering as to G, and I'm asking as to you. I'm going to ask you about G's actions as well. I'm only asking you about yours at the moment. Did you make an effort to buy the business from G? That's a yes or no question.
Objection. It's ambiguous as to what you mean by an effort. Could you maybe put some more meat on the bones for that one?
Q. (By ATTORNEY 2) Yes or no?
ATTORNEY 1: If you'd like clarification –
Q. (By ATTORNEY 2) You've told me no twice already.
A. Well, I would like clarification on – so I was trying to resolve the process in which we were going through first.
Q. Before you get to that –
ATTORNEY 1: Let her answer.
Q. (By ATTORNEY 2) – yes or no, did you make an effort to buy the business from G?

Just yes or no. Then if you answer yes or no, I'll follow up on that. But I want the primary answer to the question first.

ATTORNEY 1: Objection. First, it's asked and answered. And second -

ATTORNEY 2: Okay. You can –

ATTORNEY 1: Can you let me finish speaking, Attorney 2? Attorney 2, you are one of the rudest people I've ever encountered.

ATTORNEY 2: And you.

ATTORNEY 1: I know. And I am too, I'm sure.

I'm sure you have a great opinion of me.

That said, we're at this deposition, she's trying to give an answer, and you're interrupting her, you're interrupting me. Can we just take – just for the sake of the stenographer, can we just lighten up and take turns and pause between each other.

ATTORNEY 2: If you think your client has answered this question multiple times, why don't you tell me what the answer is.

ATTORNEY 1: I'm not testifying.

ATTORNEY 2: Then you don't know because she hasn't, so you -

ATTORNEY 1: I am not done making my objection, sir.

ATTORNEY 2: What is -

ATTORNEY 1: I am not done making my objection. I'm glad that you know what I think and -

ATTORNEY 2: What is your objection?

ATTORNEY 1: – what I do. Well, the first one was asked and answered, and the second one is that it was a vague and ambiguous question as to what you meant by effort.

My Crazy Deposition

It's the same objection that I made when you asked it first and the second time, and this is the third time. So you may not like her answer –

ATTORNEY 2: I'll ask it as many times –

– so you can ask a follow-up question.

ATTORNEY 2: Are you done yet?

ATTORNEY 1: Not yet. You can ask a follow-up question, but asking the same question over and over again, it's absurd. And so my objection, you know, also it calls for potentially hearsay, hearsay testimony.

Q. (By ATTORNEY 2) I'm going to ask the same question until you answer it.

ATTORNEY 1: Well –

Q. (By ATTORNEY 2) Did you make an effort to buy the business from G?

ATTORNEY 1: Objection. Per evidence code 765, this is asked and answered.

ATTORNEY 2: Then tell me what the answer is.

ATTORNEY 1: It's duplicative.

ATTORNEY 2: Then tell me what the answer is.

ATTORNEY 1: It's not the answer -

ATTORNEY 2: If you can tell me what the answer is, I'll move on. She hasn't answered it yet because you won't stop talking.

ATTORNEY 1: Attorney 2, could we go back to the first time and ask –

ATTORNEY 2: No. Just answer it.

ATTORNEY 1: No. You want me to answer it.

ATTORNEY 2: I'm about to stop the deposition and seek sanctions and move to continue the trial if you don't stop talking. This is my deposition. I am paying for the reporter, and 80 percent of the words on the record is yours.

ATTORNEY 1: That's not true.

ATTORNEY 2: So just make your objections and stop talking.

ATTORNEY 1: If you want to walk and cancel the deposition and seek sanctions, that is certainly, certainly your option and your right, Attorney 2.

ATTORNEY 2: And I'm real close to doing it.

ATTORNEY 1: I bet you are. But you know what -

ATTORNEY 2: Just make your – I don't care what your objection is. Just make it.

ATTORNEY 1: Just let me make my objections.

ATTORNEY 2: Make it.

ATTORNEY 1: I've already made it.

ATTORNEY 2: Fine. Stop talking.

ATTORNEY 1: But why are you getting hostile? Why are you yelling, sir?

ATTORNEY 2: Because you are –

ATTORNEY 1: Bring it down –

ATTORNEY 2: To get you to quiet down.

ATTORNEY 1: Can we go off the record?

ATTORNEY 2: No, we're going to stay on the record and finish it. Please, you've just told me you've finished with your objection. Then stop talking long enough for her to answer the question. Answer the question now, please.

ATTORNEY 1: I would like -

ATTORNEY 2: You just told me you are finished with your objection. I let you get out your whole objection. Now answer the question.

My Crazy Deposition

ATTORNEY 1: I would like to go back to her answer on the record that she made.
ATTORNEY 2: We've moved on from that.
ATTORNEY 1: No, we're not.
ATTORNEY 2: It's a yes or no question.
Q. Did you make an effort?
A. No, I did not –

> ***I did not answer this question the way I wanted to, and this was also used against me in court. It was not that I had not tried to make an offer, it was that I was trying to get G to give an amount G wanted for the business, and they would not set one.
>
> There is so much more said in these exchanges, when the attorneys are going back and forth. There is no way for the court reporter to keep up. It is so hard to sit through these exchanges, and then all of a sudden you are expected to answer.

Q. Thank you.
A. – make an effort because – I'm not finished with my answer.
ATTORNEY 1: No, no, she's not finished with her answer, Attorney 2.
ATTORNEY 2: Go ahead. Take as long as you'd like.
THE WITNESS: Are you okay? No, I did not because I thought we were finishing a process. I wasn't starting a new process until the old process was followed.

Q. (By ATTORNEY 2) Right. Did you ever make an offer to buy the business?
A. No, I did not, because according to the contract
I am supposed to allow her the opportunity when she makes an offer to purchase the company, that she's supposed to also make an offer to sell the business at the same time. That process had not been finished so I was waiting for that process to finish.

*** I tried to recover here.

Q. Did you ever make an offer to sell the business?
A. No.
Q. Did you ever make an effort to sell the business to G?

***You can see where he switches the words from "offer to" to "effort to". When the questions are being asked very fast it is so easy to miss the change in words.

ATTORNEY 1: Objection, vague and ambiguous as to what you mean by effort. If you could provide clarification, it would be appreciated.
Q. (By ATTORNEY 2) Go ahead.
ATTORNEY 1: Can you provide – if you can answer or if you'd like clarification, you can always ask for clarification. You never need to answer a question that you can't fully understand because he uses a word that's ambiguous. So if you would like clarification, feel free to. But if you feel you can answer the question without clarification, you're also free to do that. THE WITNESS: Could you please repeat the question.

Q. (By ATTORNEY 2) Did you ever make an effort to sell the business to G?
A. No. G usually –
Q. Did G –
A. Can I finish my answer?
Q. Yes, go ahead.
A. So G in this process started the initiation of making the offers. So I did not want to coGlicate things by going back and forth with too many things going on.
Q. Did G ever make an effort to buy the business from you?
A. Yes.
Q. Did G ever make an offer to buy the business from you?
A. Yes.
Q. Did G ever make an effort to sell the

business to you?
A. Yes.

> ****This was my biggest mistake, did you catch it? Two questions about buying, one question about selling, and I did not catch it. When I was asked in court "Did G ever make an offer to sell you the business?" I answered no. Attorney B called me on perjury. I was blown out of the water with this one. When I said no in court, I became guilty of perjury because I said G had offered to sell me the business in deposition. I had the physical offers that I had presented my attorneys and there was no offer to sell me the business.

Q. Did G –
A. No. I'm sorry, you're going too fast. I would like to change the answer that I just said.
Q. Did G ever make an effort to sell the business to you?

> *** I knew something was wrong. I still heard it as buy, not sell.

A. Yes.
Q. And did she make an offer to sell the business to you?
A. That sounds like the same question to me.

> ***I think this statement helped when I said it sounded the same to me. I said "You're going too fast" and "That sounds like the same question to me", and he explained it better. I

do not think Attorney 1 heard the switch, or he would have been all over it.

Q. It's very close. Effort and offer may not be the same thing.
A. So can I hear the question –
Q. The first time, I said did she make an effort; the second time, I asked did she make an offer. ATTORNEY 1: Could you just allow her to finish speaking before you interrupt. That would be helpful. THE WITNESS: G did offer, submit an offer, to sell me the business, yes.

***He did so well at talking around what he just did. He is very good at his job, I do have to give him that. He made it all about effort and offer, instead of buy or sell. I was shocked that I switched from buy to sell. I could not believe what I had just said, in my mind I heard buy.

Q. (By ATTORNEY 2) What were the terms and conditions of the offer G made to buy the business from you?

***How clever to switch back to buy.

ATTORNEY 1: Objection, calls for hearsay testimony potentially and – yeah.
Q. (By ATTORNEY 2) Go ahead.
A. Could you repeat it one more time.
Q. What were the terms and conditions of the offer G made to buy the business from you?
A. Which offer?
Q. Were there more than one?
A. Yes.

Q. How many were there?
A. I believe there were three.
Q. Okay. Tell me as to each of them.
A. The first offer was for I believe *** dollars. The terms and conditions are what I had a problem with. That's why I did not accept that offer.
Q. Okay. What were the terms and conditions as you understood them?
A. The ***** were not addressed appropriately, so that needed to be clarified in order for that amount of money to satisfy what I would have accepted as an offer for her to purchase the business. And in those offers, there was no offer for me to buy that –
Q. You just used the word "offers.". I'm only talking about one offer now. You told me there were three. I'm not asking any questions about number two or number three. Just number one.
A. Okay.
Q. So have you been answering as to number one? Because I only asked about number one.
A. Yes.
Q. Okay. So after you got offer number one and you had these various objections which you've just described –
A. Uh-huh.
Q. – did you ever make a counteroffer addressing those various objections? Yes or no, did you make a counteroffer?
A. I said the contract needed to be readdressed.
Q. Did you make a counteroffer?
ATTORNEY 1: Objection, calls for a legal conclusion as to what is a counteroffer, and also, for belated reasons, it's vague and ambiguous as to what you mean by a

counteroffer. She might not understand what is meant since it's a legal term of art.

THE WITNESS: No counteroffer was made because I was not allowed access into the company or the Vendor to see what the possible evaluation of was, the company. There was a time limit set on those offers, and they expired. Some of them were within 24 hours.

Q. (By ATTORNEY 2) Did you –

A. I'm sorry, I'm sorry.

ATTORNEY 1: Let her talk. THE WITNESS: I don't remember what the time limit on that first offer was, but it did expire.

Q. (By ATTORNEY 2) Let's talk about the second offer. What were the terms and conditions as you understood them of the second offer to buy the business from you?

A. They were the –

ATTORNEY 1: Objection, calls for potentially hearsay evidence.

THE WITNESS: It was the same exact contract with a *** dollar offer.

Q. (By ATTORNEY 2) And you had the same objections then?

A. Exactly.

Q. Did you make a counteroffer to that one?

A. I believe that expired within like 24 hours. I can't remember exactly which one expired. But there were time limits, and by the time the opportunities to try to address it, it was already expired.

Q. So whatever the time limits were, the answer is, no, you didn't make a counteroffer?

A. No.

Q. No, meaning you didn't, or, no, you're disagreeing with me? Did you make a counteroffer?

> ***I only heard one question, this last statement was an add on question.

A. I did not make a –
ATTORNEY 1: Objection, compound question.
THE WITNESS: – counteroffer because there was no offer for me to purchase the company in there as well.
Q. (By ATTORNEY 2) And what was the third offer? What were the terms and conditions of the third offer for G to buy the business from you?
ATTORNEY 1: Objection. It calls for hearsay evidence. And you can answer.
THE WITNESS: The same exact contract with the *** dollar offer, and again with no opportunity for me to purchase the business, and the same issues that were in the previous contracts.
Q. (By ATTORNEY 2) And did you make a counteroffer to that one?
A. No.
Q. What were the terms and conditions of the offer pursuant to which G proposed to sell the business to you?
ATTORNEY 1: Objection. The best evidence for this would be any written form of the offer or G's own testimony. THE WITNESS: I do not recall at this time the terms and conditions of all the – all the terms and conditions that were within that contract.
Q. (By ATTORNEY 2) How many offers were made by G to sell the business to you?

My Crazy Deposition

*** I cannot believe I still did not catch the sell. After hours of questions, they all start to sound alike. Depositions should not be allowed to last 7 hours, and this is the reason why: you get worn down. I cannot believe my attorney did not catch it as well.

A. Three.

Q. What were the terms and conditions of the first one?

A. I do not recall the exact terms and conditions of that contract.

Q. Do you recall any of the terms and conditions?

A. No.

Q. How about the second offer? Do you recall any of the terms and conditions?

A. No.

Q. How about the third?

A. No.

Q. So for three offers to sell the business to you, you have no recollection today of any of the terms and conditions?

A. No.

Q. No, meaning yes?
Yes, you have no recollection?
ATTORNEY 1: I'm sorry, you just -
ATTORNEY 2: She's answered the question.
ATTORNEY 1: Sir, look, you've asked two -you've thrown two curve balls at once. Can you just ask her one question and clarify it.

Q. (By ATTORNEY 2) Do you agree that you made no – I'm sorry, that's not what the question is – that you have no recollection of any of the terms and conditions of any of the offers pursuant to which G offered to sell the business to you?

A. I do not recall the terms and conditions at this time.

Q. And that's true as to any of the three of them?

A. Correct.

Q. In fact didn't she offer to be a buyer or a seller at the same terms and conditions?

A. She did not.

Q. Are you telling me you have never seen a proposal from her pursuant to which she said, I will sell to you or buy from you, same terms and conditions?

ATTORNEY 1: Objection. That's mischaracterizing what she said.

Q. (By ATTORNEY 2) Is that what you're telling me?

A. An offer addressed to me? I do not – I do not at this time remember her ever sending me an offer to me with that offer for me to purchase it.

> *** I said the right thing here, G never offered to sell me the business. I am not sure if the offers were entered into court as evidence. They spoke for themselves, they had no offer in them for me to purchase. In court the issue became I was out to get money for a business that was worth nothing. I was just a gold digger. G was the reasonable one, because G tried to resolve this situation with these offers. I was listening to my attorneys.

Q. That's not what I'm asking you at all. And I'm not asking whether it came from her to you. It may have come through lawyers or any other ways. What I'm asking is, are you telling me that you have no knowledge of there ever being conveyed to you a proposal pursuant to which G said she would buy the business from you or sell the business to you on the same terms and conditions?

A. At the time I do not remember that any proposal from her to me for me to purchase the business.

***I clearly said the right thing here.

Q. Again has nothing to do with what I'm asking, so let me go through it again more slowly. My client is going to testify that she told you she would be a buyer or a seller to the same terms and conditions. I'm simply asking whether you agree with that. So do you acknowledge that she ever got conveyed to you an offer to either buy or to sell under the same terms and conditions?
You can say you never heard that. That's fine.
I just want to know whether you ever heard that or not.
ATTORNEY 1: I'm going to object. It's vague and ambiguous and not – and just hope that we might be able to clarify. I understand his question, and with your permission, I maybe would like to explain it to her if that would be okay and if you agree with my statement.
ATTORNEY 2: I'll listen to it, but I don't want you testifying and you continue to try to testify for her.
ATTORNEY 1: That's fair, that's fair.
ATTORNEY 2: I'm asking a yes or no question.
ATTORNEY 1: I know. But what you're asking is a lot. Your vocabulary is so good, and it might be above some of us. So you're using big words, is basically – and I get lost.

THE WITNESS: Well, I don't see it as a yes or no answer. That's my problem.

ATTORNEY 1: So, H, with your permission

– and you can disregard this and strike it from the record. So he's asking, at any time did you receive an offer from G to both have the option perhaps of buying and/or selling for the exact same terms?

So, for example -

ATTORNEY 2: You don't have to give her an example. What you just said is fine.

ATTORNEY 1: Do you understand -

THE WITNESS: I never received an official offer with those same terms, no.

Q. (By ATTORNEY 2) So your testimony is she never said, I will either buy or sell, same terms, right?
A. I never saw that, no.
Q. After February of 2015, did you ever write another company check?
A. Yes.
Q. To whom?
A. To the mediator.
Q. Other than that?
A. No.
Q. Did you ever pay another company bill one way or the other? I don't want to limit it to checks. For example, did you ever pay a company bill?
A. Not from the business Bank account.

Did you ever do anything which you perceived increased the value of the business which you have told us you still wanted?
A. Over the entirety of the business?
Q. After February of 2015?
A. Okay. We're talking only after two thousand....

> ***The court recorder was missing things that were being said.

No.
Q. You understood that G continued to run the business after February of 2015?
A. Yes, G continued to run the business; however, she ran it alone because she had locked me out of the company by changing the passwords to the parts of the company that was how the company was run.
Q. And I realize you disagree on this, but do you understand that her perspective is that she was forced to run the business unilaterally because she concluded you abandoned it?
Is that what you understand her to be saying?
ATTORNEY 1: Objection, calls for speculation, but -
THE WITNESS: I never abandoned the company.
Q. (By ATTORNEY 2) I'm not asking you if you abandoned the company. I'm asking if you understand G to be taking the position that you abandoned the company?
A. I did not abandon the company because she locked me out. She took control of that company.
Q. I understand. That is your position.
A. Uh-huh.
Q. Obviously G disagrees with that. I'm just asking you if you understand G's position. G's position is that you abandoned the business, and I'm asking you if you understand

that that is G's position? I'm not asking you to agree with it. I'm asking if you understand that is her position?

ATTORNEY 1: Objection. Again you're asking her to speculate.

ATTORNEY 2: No, I'm asking her state of mind. I'm not asking her to speculate someone else's -

ATTORNEY 1: Her state of mind as to someone else's state of mind.

ATTORNEY 2: Right. That is not speculation.

ATTORNEY 1: That is speculation.

THE WITNESS: I cannot –

ATTORNEY 1: You're asking her –

THE WITNESS: I cannot understand -

ATTORNEY 1: – to speculate.

THE WITNESS: – how another person is thinking. I cannot think for G.

> ***With the continual interruptions, I was having difficulty staying on track with answers. There was too much going on between the two attorneys, so little was captured.

(By ATTORNEY 2) What do you believe G's disagrees with that brings us here today?

A. That I have 50 percent say in the business.

Q. You think G disagrees with that?

A. I think she disagrees with that.

Q. What is the basis of your saying you think G disagrees with that?

A. Because she locked me out of the business because I challenged G on posting *** material in a ****.

Q. Did you ever put on the website ***** without G's permission?
A. No.
Q. Did you ever pay vendor bills without G's permission?
A. No.
Q. Did you ever write checks without G's permission?
A. Yes.
Q. Why?
A. Because I didn't feel that I should solely take on the responsibility of the mediator. And if it was so decided that it was my sole responsibility, I would have paid back the other half.
Q. Are you telling me the only check you wrote without G's knowledge and consent was the check to the mediator?
A. Yes.
Q. Ever? That's the only check you've ever wrote without G's knowledge, was to the mediator?
A. That I know of. I wrote very few checks.
Q. When did this mediation take place?
A. I'm not sure of the exact date –
Q. What month?
A. – but I believe it was in March.
Q. Between the mediation and even to the present time, have you ever communicated with G?
A. No.
Q. Have you ever responded to any of G's emails?
ATTORNEY 1: Objection – oh, sorry.
THE WITNESS: G has never emailed me.
Q. (By ATTORNEY 2) You're telling me you do not have a single email to G –
A. I do not have a single –

Q. Let me finish the question.
A. I'm so sorry.
Q. You're telling me you don't have a single email to G from the time the mediation ended to the present time?
Not to me at my email address, no.
When is the last time you recall communicating with G by email?
A. I don't recall the exact date.
Q. Can you put it in the context of before this and after that, a week before the mediation or –
A. I believe the last time was mediation, before mediation.
Q. How far before mediation?
A. I don't recall the exact time frame.
Q. After you told G you had found – you did find the mediator, right?
A. Yes.
Q. After you told G you found the mediator, did you ever communicate with G again?
A. I communicated the date and the time that we were supposed to show up there.
Q. Fine.
A. After mediation –
Q. No, no, you're getting ahead of me.
A. I'm sorry.
Q. After you told G you selected a mediator, did you ever send G another email again?
A. Not that I can recall.
Q. Did you ever talk to her?
A. No.
Q. On telephone? In person?
A. No.

My Crazy Deposition

Q. Did you ever run into each other at work?
A. Yes.
Q. And you just avoided talking to each other?
A. Yes.
ATTORNEY 1: May I have a second with -
ATTORNEY 2: Sure. (Attorney A and the witness had a discussion off the record.)
ATTORNEY 1: Oh, I think that's responsive to the question.
ATTORNEY 2: Something you want to add?
ATTORNEY 1: I believe that's responsive to the question. But it also – potentially it's hearsay testimony, but I think it is responsive.
THE WITNESS: I did not communicate with G. There may have been a point when she may have said something to me, but it wasn't something that was respondable to.
Q. (By ATTORNEY 2) What was that?
A. I believe G walked by me and called me a bitch once.
Q. Was it a point when you were both at work?
I was at the telephones, and she was going to the bathroom, and G said something, and it sounded like bitch.
Q. Are you aware of any efforts that G made to ask some of your n. c. to try and interlude and help you work out your stalemate?
A. Yes.
Q. And did one or more of them come to you and say, hey, can I help you settle things?
A. One did for sure.
Q. And your response was?
A. This needs to be – this is a legal issue. This is not a work issue, and it cannot be handled here.

Q. And who was that?
A. L.
Q. And is there a reason you wouldn't just have a conversation with G and try to work it out personally?
A. I felt we did try to work it out, and I felt that we were at an impasse and that we needed somebody professional to be involved, not friends and co-workers.

> ***I made a mistake here by adding too much to this answer. I should have left it at we were at an impasse.

Q. Let's deal with that answer: I felt we had made an effort to work it out. What efforts are you describing when you say, I felt we had made an effort?
ATTORNEY 1: Objection. That calls for a narrative.
THE WITNESS: Mediation.
Q. (By ATTORNEY 2) Anything else?
A. No.
Q. So you never were willing to sit down with G and say, hey, we got a disagreement, let's talk about it?
A. I would have been willing to sit down and talk to G if G would have been acting reasonable at the time.
Q. Didn't G invite you over and over and over again to just sit down and talk with G?
ATTORNEY 1: Objection, ambiguous as to over and over and over. How many – multiple times? What are you asking? A hundred times? A thousand times? Ten times? One time? Come on.
ATTORNEY 2: Go ahead.
ATTORNEY 1: And also calls for hearsay testimony.

THE WITNESS: I still didn't feel like G was being willing to be reasonable.

Q. (By ATTORNEY 2) But how do you know if you didn't talk to her?

A. Well, because when she emails me and tells me to put my big girl panties on, it's kind of showing me that, yes, G wanted to talk to me. But if you want my big girl panties on, then I don't feel you're still willing to be reasonable about it.

Q. But wasn't that particular email in response to your saying, I hired a mediator?

A. I believe that email was after that.

Q. You told G you'd hired a mediator, and wasn't that G response, can't we just talk before you go to a mediator?

ATTORNEY 1: There's a lot of sentences in there. Object, compound. Do you understand it, or would you like it broken down? The sequence is a little off.

THE WITNESS: I'm not sure exactly of the sequence. I'm not sure that that was – I believe that was after mediation. And it wasn't just said one time.

Q. (By ATTORNEY 2) Is there a reason you didn't ask G if G would participate in mediation before G siGly went out and hired a mediator?

A. I asked her if she would participate in mediation.

ATTORNEY 1: Objection.

Q. (By ATTORNEY 2) Wasn't that after you had already hired someone?

ATTORNEY 1: Objection. I think you're reading facts into the – assuming facts that aren't in evidence.

Q. (By ATTORNEY 2) You get to answer.

A. So in the conversation we had prior to mediation, G said that I would – G would – I would never get the business, and G would shut it down before I would ever get it. In no email after that did G address any of the openness to communicate on a different level.

ATTORNEY 2: We'll mark this as Exhibit 1.

(Deposition Exhibit 1 was marked for identification.)

Q. (By ATTORNEY 2) The court reporter is showing you what we've marked as Exhibit 1. Do you agree this is an email from G to you dated February 27th, 2015?

A. I do agree.

Q. And ********* was your email address, or at least was at the time?

A. Correct.

Q. To your knowledge, did you respond to this email?

A. Yes, I did.

Q. And what was your – how did you respond? Orally? Telephone?

A. By email.

Q. Email, okay. What was your response?

A. My response to G was, if G had a solution, to go ahead and put it in writing.

Q. So in other words, you refused to sit down and meet with G? You wanted to see something in writing?

ATTORNEY 1: Objection. You're mischaracterizing what G said.

Q. (By ATTORNEY 2) G's saying in here, can we speak in person. Did you agree to speak in person with G?

A. No. I agreed for G to put G solution in writing. I was not going to meet with G without a professional witness there

My Crazy Deposition

at that point. I had already taken a lot of verbal abuse from G, and I wasn't going to take any more.

Q. What is the verbal abuse you took from G prior to February 27th?

A. The threats of –

ATTORNEY 1: Objection. It calls for hearsay testimony.

THE WITNESS: The threats of don't – don't touch buttons anymore on the website, putting my big girl panties on.

Q. (By ATTORNEY 2) And you believe that took place before February 27th?

A. Not the big girl panties. Just the way G was texting me and not allowing me to have the 50 percent say. At that point I wasn't going to allow G to

***I should have finished my statement.

-Q. In fact wasn't she trying day after day after day just to –

A. No.

Q. – try and sit down with you?

Have you ever had a disagreement with your husband?

A. Oh, yes.

ATTORNEY 1: Objection, relevance.

Q. (By ATTORNEY 2) And did you walk out of your marriage because you disagreed with him, or did you try to work it out?

ATTORNEY 1: Objection, relevance. And also I think -

THE WITNESS: It's a different situation.

ATTORNEY 1: – there's a spousal privilege that she doesn't have to disclose that information.

ATTORNEY 2: This is the next exhibit.

(Deposition Exhibit 2 was marked for identification.)

(Brief discussion was held off the record.)

Q. (By ATTORNEY 2) I'm sorry, is there something you wanted to add?

A. There's something I wanted to add.
The WTF that she had put on my *********** and the text after the ******** is the attitude that I am addressing in the –

Q. Okay. Thank you. But you already told me that was like well more than a year earlier.

A. Oh, it wasn't a year earlier.

Q. And you already told me the two of you sat down and talked it through and resolved that.

A. The ******** one, we did.

Q. Right.

A. But the ****** one was not a year prior.

Q. But when that happened, you talked it through and worked it out, right?

A. But there still was attitudes towards that.

Q. I understand.

A. Right.

Q. But you were partners with someone, you had disagreements, and each time you had a disagreement, you talked it through and worked it out, right, until this episode came up?

A. Yes.

> *** I should have said we had not worked through that issue and this issue just compounded it. In court this was just a single issue that this was over and I was just being emotional and unreasonable.

My Crazy Deposition

Q. Okay. So when this episode arises in February of 2015, G's first response to you was, let's sit down and talk about it, right?

ATTORNEY 1: Objection. I think you're assuming facts -

ATTORNEY 2: Don't testify. Make your objection.

ATTORNEY 1: No, I am going to make my objection, sir. I am objecting on the grounds that you are – it sounds like you're assuming facts that are not into evidence.

ATTORNEY 2: Fine. Make your objection.

ATTORNEY 1: If you're going to ask her -

ATTORNEY 2: Don't testify now.

ATTORNEY 1: I'm not.

ATTORNEY 2: You made your objection. After you make your objection, stop talking. Everything else is guiding her what to say.

ATTORNEY 1: It's not.

ATTORNEY 2: You've made your objection.

ATTORNEY 1: I'm trying to guide you how to ask questions.

ATTORNEY 2: Would you please answer the question.

ATTORNEY 1: If you –

ATTORNEY 2: You made your objection. The question needs an answer.

THE WITNESS: Could I please have the question again.

ATTORNEY 2: Sure. (Whereupon the last question "Okay. So when this episode arises in February of 2015, G's first response to you was, let's sit down and talk about it, right" was read back as requested.)

ATTORNEY 2: You already objected. It's time to answer.

ATTORNEY 1: Can you answer, or would you like some clarification? Or what do you want from Attorney 2?

THE WITNESS: I apologize. I didn't hear the whole question at the time. Could you please repeat it one more time. (Whereupon the last question "Okay. So when this episode arises in February of 2015, G's first response to you was, let's sit down and talk about it, right" was read back as requested again.)

THE WITNESS: So on February 27, by the time that G had sent this email at 10:16 p.m., G had that day removed the money from the account and had changed the passwords on the two business accounts, had changed the user password.

So G sent this email after G removed money from the account, half the money from the account, and changed the passwords. At that point I would not have responded to this email at ten o'clock in the evening.

Q. (By ATTORNEY 2) But you didn't respond to it at all.
A. I did respond to G after that.
Q. But that's not what the question was.

The question you still haven't answered was, after you had a disagreement, is it correct that G's first response was, let's sit down and talk about it?

That's a yes or no question. Was that G's response?

ATTORNEY 1: Objection, asked and answered, Attorney 2. You might not have liked the answer, but it was her answer. If you would like further follow-up and clarification, you can. But she did provide an answer to you.

Q. (By ATTORNEY 2) Please answer the question.
A. I thought I did. I'm sorry.
Q. You haven't answered that question.
A. The answer is, is that –

Q. I'm not asking about that. That is a different time. I acknowledge you answered that. That's not the question.

> ***He is acting like I had answered something, this was not an answer.

A. Okay. So now what's my question? I'm sorry.

> ***I was starting to lose my patience with this line of questions. He was trying to put words in my mouth and I should have said that.

Q. I think it's even before this happens.
But what I'm asking is, you had a disagreement, you recognized you had a disagreement, you came to some stalemate on it. What I'm asking is, did G say to you, let's sit down together and try to talk it out?
ATTORNEY 1: Objection, calls for hearsay testimony.
Q. (By ATTORNEY 2) Yes or no. Did G say that to you?
ATTORNEY 1: Objection. You're getting argumentative, Attorney 2. Can we just take it down a notch, please. There's no need – I think it's not advancing the ball. Can we just take it down a notch.
THE WITNESS: Yes, G asked to sit down and talk, but at the time I was waiting to consult an attorney with what G had done.
Q. (By ATTORNEY 2) Okay.
A. I was in the process of consulting an attorney from being locked out of the website and G taking half the money out before I had any conversation with G.
Q. Can you take a look at what's been put in front of you as Exhibit 2. That is also an email from G to you, correct?

A. Correct.
Q. And that one's dated March 3, 2015?
A. Correct.
Q. And am I reading it correctly where G writes: (As read) "I really think that we need to sit down and talk about our issues"?

Does G ask you that question?

ATTORNEY 1: Objection. The document speaks for itself, Attorney 2. My client doesn't need to interpret the document. If that's what it says, that's what it says.

Q. (By ATTORNEY 2) Does it say that?

ATTORNEY 1: Objection. Again that's not all it says. The document speaks for itself. THE WITNESS: I'm sorry, sir. What are you asking me? What does the document say?

Q. (By ATTORNEY 2) Does it say:

(As read) "I really think that we need to sit down and talk about our issues"?

A. The document does speak for itself, sir.
Q. And did you see that?
A. Yes, sir, I did.
Q. And did you receive it?
A. I did receive it.
Q. And did you call G in response to this?
A. There were several emails going on during that time –
Q. Did you call G –

ATTORNEY 1: Attorney 2, she was answering the question.
ATTORNEY 2: She was not.
ATTORNEY 1: You didn't let her answer the question. You didn't let her answer.
ATTORNEY 2: Listen to my question.

Q. Did you call G in response to this?
A. No, I did not call G.
Q. Did you send an email in response to this?
A. There were several emails sent with several comments in them, and I do not recall what those emails said at this time.
(Deposition Exhibit 3 was marked for identification.)
Q. (By ATTORNEY 2) The court reporter has put in front of you what's been marked as Exhibit 3. This appears to be two emails; one from you on March 3rd at 9:45 and then a response on March 3rd at 10:24.
Is that correct?
ATTORNEY 1: I'm objecting. It's really a compound question in a sense. But can we address one email at a time?
Q. (By ATTORNEY 2) Could you answer my question, please?
A. I'm sorry, sir, I was reading the email. I'm not sure what the emails say to be able to answer your question.
Q. I'll give you time to read them. I'm just identifying them first. All I asked you is, do you agree that the piece of paper in front of you includes two emails, one from you on March 3 at 9:45 p.m. and one to you on March 3 at 10:24 p.m.?
A. There are two emails on this piece of paper.
Q. The two that I just described?
I just want to make sure you understand it –
A. I'm so sorry, sir. I was reading it. I wasn't listening.
Q. All I'm asking you is, yes or no, do you agree that the piece of paper in front of you marked as Exhibit 3 includes two emails, one from you timed March 3 at 9:45 p.m., and one to you March 3 at 10:24 p.m.?

ATTORNEY 1: Objection. This is an out-of-court statement offer – well, it's being offered for the truth of the M.ers earlier, but it's potential hearsay objection.

THE WITNESS: On this piece of paper there are two emails.

ATTORNEY 2: Still doesn't answer my question.

THE WITNESS: I'm sorry.

Q. (By ATTORNEY 2) Why don't you tell me what the time and date of the two emails are.

A. I sent G an email March 3rd at 9:45, and G responded on March 3rd at 10:24.

Q. Thank you. Have you seen these before?

A. Yes.

Q. Did you respond to G's 10:24 email?

A. I do not recall that at this moment. I don't recall if I responded specifically to that email.

Q. Did you read it?

A. Yes, I've read it.

Q. And when G says in the fourth paragraph, "The splitting of the business was not my idea," did you agree with G?

A. I've never addressed splitting the business prior to this email.

Q. Again that's not my question. My question -you told me you read it. I'm just asking you, did you agree with it when you read it?

ATTORNEY 1: Objection. First of all, the document speaks for itself. You're asking her to interpret a document from a prior time and whether she agreed to something much earlier ago based on – and you're making reference to a document, another document, we haven't seen, okay.

Q. (By ATTORNEY 2) You still get to answer the question. The question doesn't change because he likes to speak.

ATTORNEY 1: I do like to speak.

THE WITNESS: On this document I do not address splitting the business.

Q. (By ATTORNEY 2) That's not what I'm asking.

You read the sentence that says, "The splitting of the business was not my idea," correct?

A. Yes.

Q. All I'm asking you is, after you read that sentence, did you agree with it?

A. I don't remember what I had thought at that time. I do not recall what I had thought of that sentence at that time.

Q. Did you ever tell G that you disagreed with that sentence?

A. I do not recall what was said in an email after this email.

Q. If you had disagreed with that, knowing yourself as you do, would you have felt obliged to respond to it and say, I don't agree with that?

ATTORNEY 1: Objection. You're asking for an iGroper hypothetical based on something that's not relevant to this M.er. She's speculating on something that is not a fact in this scenario, so. ATTORNEY 2: You still have to answer the question.

ATTORNEY 1: Actually I -

ATTORNEY 2: You made your objection.

ATTORNEY 1: Actually I'm continuing with the objection. Yeah, I'm actually instructing you not to answer that question.

ATTORNEY 2: On what basis?

ATTORNEY 1: On the form of the question.

It's an iGroper hypothetical.

Q. (By ATTORNEY 2) As a general rule in your life, when you receive an email from someone about something you disagree, do you tend to ignore it, or do you tend to say, hey, I disagree with that?

A. At this point I would not have responded to this email because I was seeking legal counsel. (Deposition Exhibit 4 was marked for identification.)

ATTORNEY 1: Give a minute to read the email first, and then we can talk about it.

Q. (By ATTORNEY 2) Ms., would you agree this is an email to you dated April 6th, 2015?

A. I agree with the date.

Q. Do you agree it's an email to you?

A. I agree it's an email to me.

Q. Did you receive this email?

A. I did receive this email.

Q. And did you read it at the time you received it?

A. Yes, sir, I did.

Q. To your recollection, did you respond to it?

A. I cannot recall at this time.

Q. So you see as you sit here today that G is saying in this email – and I'm not suggesting it's true or correct; that's sort of immaterial for purposes of the question.

G is saying, I've given you many proposals, and G's asking you to make a proposal. Did you read that when you read it? In other words, did you see that when you read it?

ATTORNEY 1: Whoa. Objection. You're asking compound questions. And the document, it speaks for itself, and she doesn't need to re-interpret a document written previously. And if she responded, she responded.

Q. (By ATTORNEY 2) Can you answer the question, please.

A. Well, I was instructed not to discuss anything that happened in mediation. So I cannot say what happened in mediation. I don't recall the date we met for mediation. At this time I was still seeking legal counsel.

Q. Did you understand that G was saying please make me a proposal when she wrote this?

A. I didn't –

ATTORNEY 1: Whoa. Objection, again, Attorney 2, the document speaks for itself. And if that's what the document says, that's what it says. And I don't think again she needs to try to interpret what she was thinking at the time about what the document states. The document either states it or doesn't.

ATTORNEY 2: To the contrary, that's exactly what you need to do. I'm asking you your state of mind when you read this, and I'm entitled to that.

Q. So after you read this and you saw G write to you, please make a proposal, first question is, did you read it?

A. Yes, sir.

Q. And did you make a proposal?

A. I was still seeking legal counsel, and I did not – had not had that opportunity to coGlete that, so I did not respond to this email.

Q. So you just told me you didn't respond to the email. Did you at any time – and "you" means you or somebody on your behalf, including a lawyer. Did you at any time make a proposal?

A. No. From this email, no. From this email, no.
I'm sorry, could we just step out for five minutes? It's getting awfully warm in here.

> ***This room was starting to become unbearably hot. It started to affect the way I was thinking, and I needed to physically get out of the heat.

ATTORNEY 2: Sure, absolutely. Let's just take a couple minutes. (Recess taken from 2:10 p.m. to 2:20 p.m.)

> ***At this point I still had hours left of this.

(Deposition Exhibit 5 was marked for identification.)
Q. (By ATTORNEY 2) Ms., the reporter has put in front of you what I guess is marked as Exhibit 5. Do you have that?
A. Yes.
Q. And am I correct in describing this as an email of March 3rd, 2010?
Just asking you to agree to the date.
A. Oh, I'm so sorry. Yes, sir, March 3rd.
Q. 2010?
A. 2010, yes.
Q. And this is an email from G to you?
A. This is an email from G to me.
Q. So this is written from her to you at the time she was first talking to you about going into business together?
A. Can I read the email?
Q. Sure.
ATTORNEY 1: Objection.
ATTORNEY 2: Sure, absolutely.
Q. Have you had a chance to read that?
A. Yes, sir.
Q. Does that refresh your recollection that in fact
G came to you with the idea of running a business together?

A. Could you please rephrase the question – or not rephrase. Could you please clarify the question for me.
ATTORNEY 1: Yeah, what was the question?
Q. (By ATTORNEY 2) What is it you don't understand?
I asked you earlier if you remember whether it was G's idea or your idea to go into this business, and you seemed to infer that it was either yours or a joint effort. And what I'm asking you now is, does this refresh your recollection that in fact it was G's idea?
You can say no if you don't.
A. I'll say no. I don't think this insinuates that G is the only person that was involved in starting this business.
Q. No, I'm not talking about starting the business.
I'm talking the concept for the business. Long before someone starts it, it generates as an idea in somebody's head, and I'm asking you if this refreshes your recollection that that idea came from G?
A. I do not recall.
(Deposition Exhibit 6 was marked for identification.)
Q. (By ATTORNEY 2) Let me show you what we've marked as Exhibit 6.
ATTORNEY 1: Thank you, sir.
Q. (By ATTORNEY 2) Exhibit 6 is also two emails, one from you to G March 4, 2010 which appears to probably be a response to Exhibit 5, and then G's further response dated March 5, 2010. Take a second and read those if you'd like. Have you had a chance to read that?
A. I'm not finished, sir.
Q. Okay.
(Brief discussion was held off the record.)

> ***I cannot recall what would have been discussed off the record.

Q. (By ATTORNEY 2) Okay? H?
A. I'm not quite finished, sir. I'm rereading a couple things, please.
Q. Well, I don't have that many questions, so it may make more sense to hear the question and then read all you want.
A. Okay. Well, I want to finish this.
Q. That's fine.
A. Okay, sir.
Q. So we've already established that G sent you an email on March 3 which is Exhibit 5. Do you agree that the earlier of the two emails on Exhibit 6 written March 4th was your response to that?
ATTORNEY 1: Objection. I don't –
THE WITNESS: I do not recall this email being a response to that email. I believe there was other conversations going on, and part of that may be with conversations that were held outside of these emails.
Q. (By ATTORNEY 2) Okay. So on March 4th, you wrote this five-paragraph email to G, and right in the first paragraph you wrote, "I have to know why you" – I'm sorry.
(As read) "I have to know why would you pick me to take on such a big endeavor."
Does that refresh your recollection that the idea of running a business together was G's, not yours?
A. That does not say that to me in that sentence.
The way I was saying – meaning this to say was in a bigger thought of, what was it about me that G was picking

to go into business about. I was articulating before we move forward, why we were – why we were getting in this together – I wanted to slow things down and kind of articulate things before we move forward.

Q. But you just used the phrase: Why G was picking me to go into business together. So did G come to you and say, let's do something together?

A. No.

Q. Then why do you think G picked you, your words?

ATTORNEY 1: Objection. I think this is vague and ambiguous in your use -

ATTORNEY 2: Fine. You made your objection.

ATTORNEY 1: Vague of the word "picking."

Could you please clarify what you mean by picking, and then see if it's the same that Ms. means.

Q. (By ATTORNEY 2) Go ahead.

A. Picking didn't mean that to me in this particular email. It was – "picking" probably was a poor choice of words. But my intention was, is why would you want to go into business with me.

Q. Okay. That's fine. So which of you do you recall going to the other first and saying, let's go into business together? Someone had to start that conversation.

ATTORNEY 1: She asked and answered that much earlier.

THE WITNESS: G.

Q. (By ATTORNEY 2) G asked it of you?

ATTORNEY 1: Asked and answered.

Q. (By ATTORNEY 2) Is that what you're saying? G asked you?

A. If I would like to go into business?

Q. Yes.

A. Yes.

Q. Okay. Turning to this second page of Exhibit 6 on the third paragraph of this email, why did you write the phrase: (As read) "Setting this business up in your home has some responsibilities with it"?

ATTORNEY 1: Objection. The document speaks for itself. The document -

THE WITNESS: The document speaks for itself, but the business wasn't being set up in her house. I know that's the terminology that I used, but this was like the second day, and that's not what we decided on at a later date. We would each have our own in-home – the website was the business, and our – each of our homes would have its own in-home office. There was no – her house was not a business you walked into and did business. That was articulated between us later at a later date, that the documents would be held at her house because she had an office in her home, but that the business was the website, and we had our own in-home offices.

Q. (By ATTORNEY 2) Do you agree that you told G that this would probably end up being G business?

A. I do remember telling her that, yes –

Q. And it says that –

A. – because I was older.

Q. And it says that in here?

A. I do remember saying that, yes.

Q. And you said it in this email, right?

ATTORNEY 1: Where are you referencing? I'm sorry.

ATTORNEY 2: Third paragraph.

THE WITNESS: On which page, sir?

My Crazy Deposition

Q. (By ATTORNEY 2) Second page, first full paragraph of the second page.

ATTORNEY 1: First full paragraph?

THE WITNESS: Yes.

Q. (By ATTORNEY 2) And you also point out to G at the end in the last couple lines, "By the way I'm an awful speller."

A. Yeah, I admit to being an awful speller. That's why I wrote on Computers, because Computers do a lot of spell check.

Q. When you wrote ****, did you use the ***** checks?

A. Absolutely. But that doesn't mean that every word is corrected properly. In fact it sometimes changes it to different words.

(Deposition Exhibit 7 was marked for identification.)

Q. (By ATTORNEY 2) Let me show you what's been marked as Exhibit 7, and we don't really have to reread Exhibit 7 because all of Exhibit 6 is on Exhibit 7. The only thing that is new is the top couple paragraphs. So in the top paragraph dated March 8, 2010, an email from G to you, G says:

(As read) "I hope you like the business name. I went with The Business."

Does that refresh your recollection that **** came up with the name, not you?

A. I came up with the name "My Business". The "additions to the name" was added.

Q. So notwithstanding what's written here, you think you came up with the name?

A. I came up with the name "My Business". That's what I've always said. I came up with the name "My Business". G added the other. G added that on G own when G went down to the county to apply for the business license.

Q. When you were first – let me back up a little before I change topics on you here. When you complained to G that G had used those various **** that you thought were * protected, and you ***** the site and then G ***** the site, when **** reactivated the site, hadn't **** taken down the pictures you objected to?
A. Not the first time.
Q. What does that mean?
A. That means **** just reactivated the course, the same exact course the first time.
Q. And so it sounds like you're saying *** reactivated a **** time without those pictures?
A. G reactivated it – I don't know when G reactivated the second time, because at that point I was locked out of the company.
Q. You could have gotten onto the website whether or not you were purportedly locked out, right?
ATTORNEY 1: Objection. That's assuming -that's a hypothetical. That's really iGroper. That wasn't her answer, and it's really irrelevant whether or not she could have or not.
ATTORNEY 2: Don't testify. Just object.
ATTORNEY 1: No, sir, I'm objecting.
THE WITNESS: You asked me when G reactivated it, did I know if the **** were entered or not?
Q. (By ATTORNEY 2) Correct.
A. And when *** did it at that time, I did not know whether or not those ***** were on there.
Q. Did you check?

> ***In court he rephrased the question, and I should have answered that question differently.

My Crazy Deposition

It was because of this line of questioning he was able to do that.

A. Later on I did, and the images were removed.
But the grammerical errors had not been corrected.
Q. So it sounds like –
A. There was nothing I could do – I'm sorry, may I coGlete that answer?
Q. Sure.
A. However, when G reactivated the second time, there was nothing I could do about it anyway because I was locked out of the company.
Q. But it sounds like you raised a concern, G heard your concern, G addressed your concern by doing exactly what you asked for. G took down what you thought were ******, right?

ATTORNEY 1: Objecting on the grounds of it being compound.

ATTORNEY 2: Fine. Go ahead and answer.

ATTORNEY 1: Could you please break it down.
What is your question? Everything in front of it, or is it just the last part? What do you want her to answer?

Q. (By ATTORNEY 2) Do you understand the question?
A. Could you please repeat the question.

ATTORNEY 2: Sure. Could you repeat the question, please. (Whereupon the question "But it sounds like you raised a concern, she heard your concern, she addressed your concern by doing exactly what you asked for. G took down what you thought were *******, right" was read back as requested.)

ATTORNEY 2: You already objected. It's time to answer.

ATTORNEY 1: I would like clarification on the compound question.

THE WITNESS: So the answer –

ATTORNEY 2: She knows -

ATTORNEY 1: She can answer an individual question.

ATTORNEY 2: There's only one question.

ATTORNEY 1: It was a compound question of like four questions.

ATTORNEY 2: Go ahead.

ATTORNEY 1: But if you feel you can answer it or if you would like to address each specific, please feel free to do that.

THE WITNESS: So, no, G did not address all the issues that were wrong with that particular *****. There was more than just the ******. So G did not address all the concerns I had with that *****, even though I was locked out of the business and could not correct those other issues that – or have those other issues corrected. At that point I had no access.

Q. (By ATTORNEY 2) And the other issues are what you perceived to be a couple of spelling or grammatical errors?

A. No. It was no page numbers, grammerical errors, misspellings and spacing issues. And the rest, I may not recall.

ATTORNEY 1: Can I have -

ATTORNEY 2: The question is answered.

ATTORNEY 1: Can I just have a second with my client? Thank you, sir. (Attorney A and the witness had a discussion off the record.)

THE WITNESS: Oh, uh-huh.

ATTORNEY 1: I don't know. Is there anything else?

THE WITNESS: The other issue that was discussed was the course was only for a certain amount of ****, was offered for a larger amount of ****than we had agreed to in the past for the amount of words per ****, and that also needed to be addressed as well.
Q. (By ATTORNEY 2) Did you ever raise that with G?
A. Yes. It was in that – all that correction sheets that I had sent to G.
Q. So going back to your point in time where now you're starting this business in April of 2010, did you ask G at some point, hey, do you want a partnership agreement?
A. You're talking about the legal document, sir?
Q. Yes, a legal agreement.
A. I had told G that we would do things legally and that we needed to get something into writing.
Q. Do you recall *** saying you didn't need one?
A. *** says, well, I don't think we need one, but whatever you think.
Q. And then you produced what became the partnership agreement? You've already told us that, right?
A. Yes, sir.
  (Deposition Exhibit 8 was marked for identification.)
Q. (By ATTORNEY 2) The document that is in front of you is Exhibit 8. Do you agree that is the partnership agreement we've been talking about?
A. Yes, sir.
Q. This is the document that you came up with that you both signed? I'm just asking you to authenticate the document.
A. I'm just going through it, sir, please.
ATTORNEY 1: Yes, just allow her to review it so that she can actually verify that it is the document purported to be.

THE WITNESS: Yes, sir.

Q. (By ATTORNEY 2) And it looks like you signed it on April 12th and G on April 13th, 2010?

A. Yes, sir.

Q. Any reason to recall differently?
Or that's when you think it was signed?

A. We worked different shifts so we would have signed it at different times.

Q. I'm just asking, to your best recollection today, do you believe those are the dates on which it was signed?

A. Yes, sir.

Q. So when you wrote this, looking at paragraph four, am I correct that you wrote that the main office of the partnership would be in G's home?

ATTORNEY 1: Objection. I think you're -the document speaks for itself. I think it's specifically – we haven't identified this as G's home. Is that – I think you're reading facts in that are not there.

Q. (By ATTORNEY 2) Please answer the question.

ATTORNEY 1: If you know it to be G's home, you can answer it.

THE WITNESS: The reason why we called it the main office is because we agreed that the documents for the business would reside there.

Q. (By ATTORNEY 2) And that is G's home?

A. Correct.

Q. And you agree that you wrote in paragraph six that you would each make a capital contribution of a thousand dollars?

A. Correct.

Q. And you told me you did that, correct?

A. Yes, sir. I'm sorry.
Q. What is your understanding of the capital account?
A. That that is a way of partners being equal in the start-up costs or the agreed amount that would be the partnership funds for that account.
Q. Okay. A capital account is a legal term of art in partnership law. You have written a partnership agreement in which you describe a capital account. So what I would like you to tell me is what your understanding of a capital account is, whether or not it's right, whether or not it's legal?
I just want to know what your understanding was when you wrote this in 2010. ATTORNEY 1: Objection. The document speaks for itself as to what the capital account is, and I don't – I think you're calling for a legal conclusion also. Whether or not you want a legal definition or not, you're still -
ATTORNEY 2: I'm just asking for her understanding.
THE WITNESS: My understanding has changed over time. I cannot tell you -Q.　(By ATTORNEY 2) First, what was it then?

> ***I should have said I do not recall what I thought at that time, and stayed with that answer. Many of these same questions were brought up in court.

A. I do not recall.
ATTORNEY 1: Can you let her answer her question.
Q. (By ATTORNEY 2) What is your understanding now?
A. That that is the funds that partnerships deposit in for a business for it to be represented as 50 percent.

Q. So do you believe there are no capital accounts if you have unequal partners?
A. I don't know that.
ATTORNEY 1: Objection, calls for a legal conclusion.
Q. (By ATTORNEY 2) Is it fair to say you got this language from some form and made no effort to interpret it one way or the other?
ATTORNEY 1: Objection. You're reading facts into the record that don't exist here. You're assuming these facts are in evidence. They're not. You're putting together a legal conclusion and asking her to agree with it.
ATTORNEY 2: Just make an objection.
ATTORNEY 1: You're asking her – I don't even know what the question is.
ATTORNEY 2: That's not an objection. Just tell us what your objection is, because everything else is testimony. Tell us what your objection is.
ATTORNEY 1: It's not. My objection is the full statement that I'm making. Could you please reread the question so I can hear it. And if I have to withdraw the objection, I will. But I'd like to rehear the question.
(Whereupon the last question "Is it fair to say you got this language from some form and made no effort to interpret it one way or the other" was read back as requested.)
ATTORNEY 1: I'd also like to add that it's a compound question. You got it from some form, is one question, and made no atteGt to interpret it, is a whole other question. Can we break it down one at a time?
ATTORNEY 2: No.
Q. You can answer.
A. Could you please clarify that question.

My Crazy Deposition

Q. Sure. Is it fair to say you just took this language out of a form?

A. No, sir, that is not fair to say that.

Q. So if you didn't take it out of a form, that means you wrote it, right?

A. It came as a basic form with fields that you were supposed to add in, and I had read the instructions that came with it and tried to be pro active on doing this as accurately for that date that I possibly could.

Q. But you also told me that in 2010 you didn't know what a capital account was.

A. I did not say that, sir. That's not what I said.

Q. So what was your understanding of a capital account in 2010 when you wrote this language?

A. What I told you, sir, was I can't remember what my thoughts around it were at that time.

Q. But it is your testimony you wrote that language?

A. I did write that language.

> ***What I should have said was, I filled in the available fields with the available information of that date.

Q. Okay. In paragraph 8.B., you have this provision that the partnership will make distributions to the partners only if all of the partners agree. Did you ever take money out of the partnership without asking G to agree?
ATTORNEY 1: Objection. The document speaks for itself as far as what it says. And my objection as to taking money out, I don't believe there's a proper foundation for that.
ATTORNEY 2: Just answer the question.

ATTORNEY 1: Out of what account? It's also ambiguous as to what account you're talking about. Are you referring to the capital account or another account? There's also a PayPal account. And it's not limited as to the time when you're asking. Are you asking ever or during the life of the partnership, or are you asking this particular year in 2010 at the time this was drafted? What are you asking? Could you please provide clarification.

Q. (By ATTORNEY 2) Answer the question, please.
A. Could you please clarify that question.
Q. Did you ever take any funds out of the partnership without G's consent?
A. Yes, once, and that was the funds for the mediation.
Q. And you're telling me that's the only time it ever happened?
A. That's the only time it ever happened.
Q. When you wrote paragraph 11, what did you mean by the word "routine"?
A. Could I go back to my answer on that?
Q. Sure.
A. Could you please reread that question.
Q. I'm just asking if you ever took money out of the account, and you said just one time.
A. No. What was the question again, please.
(Whereupon the question "Did you ever take any funds out of the partnership without G's consent" was read back as requested.)
Q. (By ATTORNEY 2) And you've said just one time. Anything to add?
A. Yes, let's leave that answer.
Q. So moving to paragraph 11, when you wrote that, what did you mean by the word "routine"?

A. Every day-to-day issues that might arise that we both would make a decision about.
Q. Well, you didn't say "every." Using an adjective like "routine" –
A. So, sir –
ATTORNEY 1: Stop, stop, stop. Let him talk. Let him talk.
ATTORNEY 2: Let me ask the question.
Q. Using an adjective like "routine" in front of "decisions" infers there's some decisions excluded from this. That may be what you meant; it may not. So I'm asking you what you meant by routine as opposed to something that was not routine. Because if you meant any, why didn't you say "any"?
ATTORNEY 1: Objection. The document speaks for itself, and you're asking her to interpret a document that's like, what, seven years old, what she meant at that particular time at that specific time. I don't see how this is -
ATTORNEY 2: Answer the question, please.
ATTORNEY 1: If you can answer the question, if you know what he's saying or if you recall.
THE WITNESS: I don't recall all my thoughts around why that language was left in place. The reason why the "routine" was left is because at that time I didn't know all – what all decisions could possibly come up in the future.
Q. (By ATTORNEY 2) Do you agree that you wrote paragraph 14?
A. I did not write paragraph 14. Most of that language was preloaded with that program.
Q. Did you write paragraph 16?

ATTORNEY 1: Give me – I'm sorry. Can I have just a second to look at 14. Okay, go ahead. I'm sorry. Please proceed.

THE WITNESS: If the first part of that paragraph was the Computer program, kind of preloaded that one. I did add in the next two sentences.

Q. (By ATTORNEY 2) Meaning the second paragraph of 16?

A. Actually I believe the – I do not recall putting that in there other than:

(As read) "If H chooses to leave the partnership, the business may or will continue without her. It would not need to close." And that was in reference to retiring.

Q. The question was, did you write paragraph 16?

A. I did not write all of paragraph 16.

ATTORNEY 1: I'm sorry –

Q. (By ATTORNEY 2) Did you write the second paragraph of paragraph 16?

ATTORNEY 1: Objection. It's ambiguous and vague as to the meaning of write. I think there might be some confusion as to what is meant by your question. Could you perhaps provide additional clarification.

Q. (By ATTORNEY 2) Go ahead and answer.

Did you write the second paragraph of paragraph 16?

A. I do not recall writing the first part of that sentence. I did write, "If H chooses to leave" -I do remember writing:

(As read) "If H chooses to leave the partnership, the business may or will continue without her.

It will not need to close." And that was in reference to retiring.

Q. Going back to paragraph 14, as you sit here today, do you agree that the first sentence of paragraph 14 and the

My Crazy Deposition

second sentence of paragraph 14 can be inconsistent with each other? ATTORNEY 1: Objection, calling for a legal conclusion. And also I would have to say that the document speaks for itself, and it's vague and ambiguous as to what you mean by inconsistent.

Could you please provide additional clarification.

ATTORNEY 2: You've made your objection. We're waiting for her to answer. Don't answer for her. ATTORNEY 1: I'm not. I'm trying to help her.

ATTORNEY 2: You've made your objection.

Q. Go ahead and answer the question.

ATTORNEY 1: If you feel you can answer it, answer it. If you feel you need further clarification, you do not need to answer a question that you don't understand. So if you want Attorney 2 to provide more clarification, he is certainly capable of doing that, and he should do that in my opinion.

THE WITNESS: Could you please repeat the question.

Q. (By ATTORNEY 2) I'm just asking, do you agree that those two sentences can be inconsistent with each other?

A. I don't read them to be inconsistent. I read them to be kind of what the document says.

Q. Okay. So in the first sentence we have a potential arising from the withdrawal of a partner that says upon withdrawal of the partner, the other partners will make some decision. Do you see that?

A. Yes.

Q. And the second sentence says a decision requires unanimous consent, where the first sentence says the other partners will decide. So if one says the other partners will decide and the second says there's unanimous consent, do you agree that's potentially inconsistent?

ATTORNEY 1: Objection. That's a compound question. It's also vague and ambiguous as to what you mean by inconsistent. Also you're reading – object as to you're reading the sentences out of the full context of the document and trying to have her interpret it which is – which would be a legal conclusion. Those are my objections.

Q. (By ATTORNEY 2) It's siGly a yes, no or you don't know.
A. Could you please repeat the question.
Q. I'm just asking if there's a potential they're inconsistent, and I just highlighted what the inconsistency is. Would you like me to highlight it again?

ATTORNEY 1: I think she's answered this question already.
THE WITNESS: I don't believe there's an inconsistency with the language.

Q. (By ATTORNEY 2) Okay. Do you understand what a coGlaint is, the coGlaint that begins a lawsuit?
A. Yes, sir.
Q. A coGlaint is the name that we give the document which starts a lawsuit.
A. Yes, sir.
Q. And when your attorney drafted the coGlaint, did you read it?
A. Yes, sir.
Q. And did you agree with the factual allegations which were contained in the coGlaint?
A. At that time, yes.

ATTORNEY 1: Objection.
ATTORNEY 2: She answered the question.
ATTORNEY 1: Yes, she did.

My Crazy Deposition

Q. (By ATTORNEY 2) Were you given an opportunity to edit or amend the coGlaint if you thought something was incorrect?

A. Yes.

Q. And to your recollection, did you make any changes?

A. I do not recall.

Q. But at the end of the process, whether you made changes or not, before it was filed you acknowledged that what was in there you believed at that time to be true and correct?

A. Yes, sir.

Q. So you have alleged that G failed to provide you with a partnership accounting. What do you feel you did not get?

A. I did not have access to the accounts to be able to understand what was going on within the business. So I could not – I could not keep track of what was going on in the Vendor. I had no idea of what was going on in the web part of the business. After April, I had no idea what was going on in the PayPal account. So I had no idea what any kind of financial items were going on at that time.

Q. Are you aware of any persons other than yourself who have knowledge of that which you described in that answer?

A. Could you please clarify that question.

Q. Sure. You're saying – I had asked you before what you believe G failed to do, and you just told me.

A. Uh-huh.

Q. And I'm asking who you think is aware of those facts other than you obviously and G.

A. I know J at Vendor is aware. I know that M. is aware. PayPal, there's not like a specific person you can communicate with. My husband is aware; not of

what's in those accounts but the fact that G had locked me out. Is that what you're asking me?
Q. Well, I'm talking about partnership accounting, your words in the coGlaint. You said that G failed or refused to give you a partnership accounting. And I'm just looking for who the persons are who have knowledge of this failure to provide an accounting.
A. J, M.. There's not a physical person at PayPal.
Q. Anyone else you can think of?
A. Not that I can recall at this time.
Q. You characterize G's operation of the partnership as waste. Do you know what waste of partnership assets means? And again I realize lawyers write coGlaints, but they're words clients eventually adopt. So do you know what it means when you allege that my client wasted partnership or engaged in waste of partnership assets?
A. I do not recall the full explanation that was given to me at that time.
Q. Are you aware of anything which you believe constitutes waste of partnership assets?
ATTORNEY 1: Objection. The question does call for potentially attorney/client privileged communication. So to the extent -
THE WITNESS: I did discuss that with my attorney.
Q. (By ATTORNEY 2) I'm not asking you about any of your conversations with your lawyer. I'm asking of your personal knowledge. Do you have any personal knowledge of facts, circumstances or other things which you believe constitutes waste of partnership assets? ATTORNEY 1: I wasn't done with my objection when you interjected. But again to the extent that you can answer the question without disclosing

attorney/client privileged communication, answer his question.
THE WITNESS: Yes.

> ***I know the attorneys explained that they had filed this paperwork, and sent me a copy. They did not go over every single word of what they had put in the filing. I was not sure how I was going to answer these questions, and should have answered, "I do not recall".

Q. (By ATTORNEY 2) What?
A. I do not recall at that time that was filed what was discussed between the attorneys and me.
Q. I'm not asking about anything that was discussed with your lawyers. I'm asking your personal knowledge. You lived this. So in your head there's some belief that G did something iGroper. I'm trying to learn what you think G did that you think was iGroper. So what I'm asking you is, what of the actions G undertook do you believe constituted waste of partnership assets?
A. She locked me out of the accounts.
Q. How did that waste partnership assets?

> ***Here is where I should have talked about the money G spent without my consent.

A. Because I did not have access in order to help grow the business. I did not have the ability to continue to advertise on the Marketing page. I did not have the opportunity to be involved with continuing our business to become successful.

Q. Okay. So let me ask an example.
If the business in 2014 had made a hundred bucks and the business in 2015 after you're locked out had made a million bucks and all the same facts were there where you believe you were locked out, does that in your mind still constitute waste of partnership assets when the business made more money after you were locked out?

ATTORNEY 1: Objection, calls for an iGroper hypothetical.

THE WITNESS: I'm going to defer to my attorney on that one.

Q. (By ATTORNEY 2) Do you understand what I'm asking you?
A. I do, but I –
Q. If you understand it, you've got to answer it.
You can't keep looking to him before answering the questions.
A. I would like to ask him a question on the process. If I don't really understand what's being asked in the question, can I just say -

ATTORNEY 2: Absolutely.

ATTORNEY 1: Ask for clarification, absolutely, yeah.

THE WITNESS: Okay. I don't understand what the question is asking.

Q. (By ATTORNEY 2) Is the problem that you don't know what waste is? That's my perception, is that you don't know what lawyers mean when they use the word "waste."
A. I am not an attorney.
Q. That's why I understand that.
A. And I cannot always understand what attorneys are saying.

Q. So is it fair to say when your lawyer used the word "waste" of partnership assets, you don't know what it means?
ATTORNEY 1: Objection. That's -
ATTORNEY 2: It would shorten this a whole lot if you would just tell me that.
ATTORNEY 1: – potentially attorney/client privileged communication. Also I'm instructing you to the extent that it contains privileged communication, not to answer that. But perhaps you can
Q. (By ATTORNEY 2) I'm asking you what you know.
A. I don't understand the question enough to give you
Q. And is that because you don't understand use of the word "waste" in this context?
A. I don't understand how you're asking me – I don't understand what you're looking for in that question.
Q. I'm just looking at allegations you made, and I'm trying to learn what the facts are which support those allegations. So one of those allegations is, G engaged in waste of partnership assets. You wrote that. I realize your lawyer wrote it, but you adopted it, and you filed something with that allegation. I'm entitled to ask you what you mean when you say G engaged in waste of partnership assets.
If your answer is, I don't know because my lawyer wrote it, just tell me that and I'll move on. But if you don't tell me that, you have to answer the question.
ATTORNEY 1: I'm so sorry. Can we just for one second – again I'm reasserting attorney/client privilege and recommending you not answering to the extent that it might be confidential attorney/client communication. But perhaps if you provide her a copy of the coGlaint so she can see what she wrote or what was written on her behalf and

confirmed, it will refresh her recollection, and she will have a better, easier time of answering your question rather than turning her into a punching bag over whether she understands or ever understood the definition of legal waste. I would – I just think that would be a better way to go, Attorney 2, if you are amenable to that.

Q. (By ATTORNEY 2) Can you answer the question, please. I assume the answer is you don't know. You just have to tell me that if that's the answer.

A. I don't know that. I don't know because I don't understand really what you're asking. I feel like –

Q. Okay. I'll be glad to ask it again.

A. – you're asking me a question that whatever I answer is – I can't say everything that –

Q. Let me back up and explain.

My job is to learn what facts are in your head. You have made allegations. I want to know what those allegations are. So I'm asking you to tell me what the facts are. If there's something you don't know the answer to or there is no answer, you're perfectly entitled to just tell me that. But one of the allegations you put in the lawsuit is G engaged in waste of partnership assets. If you don't know what those words mean, then you don't have to answer my question. But what I'm asking you, if you do know what those words mean, is, what did you mean when you adopted an allegation that G engaged in waste?

A. Can I just say I do not recall at this time?

Q. That's fine.

ATTORNEY 1: That's perfectly fine.

THE WITNESS: I just want to say I do not recall at this time.

My Crazy Deposition

Q. (By ATTORNEY 2) I don't assume you know, but you've got to tell me if you don't know.

A. You cannot assume what I know or don't know.

ATTORNEY 1: Objection, Attorney 2. I think you're mischaracterizing what just transpired. I think you were trying to say that she did not know what was written at the time or it wasn't explained to her by her attorney.

ATTORNEY 2: Stop testifying.

ATTORNEY 1: But it is attorney/client privileged communication.

ATTORNEY 2: Stop testifying.

ATTORNEY 1: I'm not.

ATTORNEY 2: You are testifying.

ATTORNEY 1: I'm not testifying.

ATTORNEY 2: You've been subpoenaed. You will get your chance to testify. It's not today.

> ***I heard this but it did not register that they had subpoenaed my attorney. I was shocked to find out my attorney could be subpoenaed for G's side. When this came up in court I could not believe it. Attorney 1 was never called to the stand.

ATTORNEY 1: You can get me subpoenaed, sir, like you lost that ex parte this morning.

> ***It was obvious he was extremely upset about this. He had filed paperwork, and I actually had to be at the court house before this deposition started to file paperwork in response to this ex parte. This day started at 7 AM for me at the

> court house. It was actually going to be a 9 hour day. He was furious he lost this ex parte.

Q. (By ATTORNEY 2) Anyway you used the phrase that G engaged in waste of partnership opportunities. Do you know what that phrase means?

ATTORNEY 1: Objection, calls for –

Q. (By ATTORNEY 2) Yes or no. Do you know what that means?

ATTORNEY 1: Can I make my objection?

ATTORNEY 2: No, because you don't know how to make an objection.

ATTORNEY 1: I'm not allowed to make an objection?

ATTORNEY 2: You are allowed to make objections. You are –

ATTORNEY 1: Attorney 2 -

ATTORNEY 2: – not allowed to testify.

ATTORNEY 1: – this is really getting old.

ATTORNEY 2: Then make an objection.

ATTORNEY 1: I did. Hearsay is not an objection? Is that not an objection?

ATTORNEY 2: It is not actually.

ATTORNEY 1: You're saying it's not an objection?

ATTORNEY 2: It's not allowed in a deposition.

ATTORNEY 1: It is to preserve your right to -

ATTORNEY 2: Hearsay is not.

ATTORNEY 1: I tend to differ on that one, but -

ATTORNEY 2: Well, you would be wrong.

ATTORNEY 1: – that's quite all right.

ATTORNEY 2: You'd be wrong.

ATTORNEY 1: Wait. Are you –

ATTORNEY 2: Just make an objection.

ATTORNEY 1: Out-of-court statements offered for the truth of the M.er asserted, you're saying that there are no out-of-court statements -

ATTORNEY 2: Make an objection.

ATTORNEY 1: – based on comments that you're asking whether your client made? Maybe there might be an exception, sure, but it's a proper objection -

ATTORNEY 2: Make your objection.

ATTORNEY 1: – hearsay. And also as I said before, potentially attorney/client privileged communication.

ATTORNEY 2: Answer the question now, please.

ATTORNEY 1: To the extent that you can. And I am instructing -

> ***There was so much more said, but it was all being said so fast that there was no way everything could have been captured.

THE WITNESS: Could you please reread the question.

Q. (By ATTORNEY 2) The question is very simple. You alleged – you are alleging that G engaged in waste of partnership opportunities. That's what the allegation is. Do you know what that means?

A. I do not recall –

ATTORNEY 1: It's asked and answered, asked and answered.

THE WITNESS: – what the attorneys explained to me at that time.

Q. (By ATTORNEY 2) I'm not asking what they explained to you. Do you – as you sit here right now, do you know what those words mean?

A. At this moment I do not recall what the attorneys explained to me at that time.

Q. Do you know what the words mean, whether they explained them to you or not?
ATTORNEY 1: I don't think –

Q. (By ATTORNEY 2) I'm not asking what they explained to you. You are sitting here right now in 2017. Do you know what those words mean?
ATTORNEY 1: Which words?
THE WITNESS: What words are you asking me, sir?

Q. (By ATTORNEY 2) Engaged in waste of partnership opportunities.
ATTORNEY 1: You can answer his question if you know what -
THE WITNESS: Yes, I feel I knew at that time what was being said.

Q. (By ATTORNEY 2) And what was the waste of partnership opportunities?

A. Could I please see the document.

Q. There's no document. I'm just asking you a question -
ATTORNEY 1: She's already –
THE WITNESS: I do not recall –
(Reporter interruption.)

> ***The reporter interrupted because it was getting crazy with the constant going back and forth. There was so much more said in this exchange that was not able to be documented. No one should have to put up with hours of this type of questioning, unless it is when you

are in the an interrogation room for a crime. He was still angry I think over losing the ex parte. They should only allow this process to be a few hours so attorneys have to ask a question, and get an answer whether they like it or not and move on.

I should have said without seeing the document, I cannot answer the question.

Q. (By ATTORNEY 2) I'm just asking you a question. I don't have to show you things. If he wants to show you things, he can ask you questions and show you what he wants.
A. I do not recall. I do not recall.
ATTORNEY 1: Let's move on. She's answered the question.
Q. (By ATTORNEY 2) ·What don't you recall?
A. I do not recall.
ATTORNEY 1: Objection. You're asking an illogical iGossibility of her explaining a negative. I don't know what "I don't know" – sorry.
Q. (By ATTORNEY 2) You've accused G of mismanaging the partnership. Is there anything you believe G did to mismanage the partnership that you haven't already told us?
A. Shutting down the business.
Q. Anything else?
A. Spending funds that were not approved through the partnership. All money that was spent that were not approved through the partnership I feel were mismanaged funds.
Q. Anything else?

A. Closing of the MarketingI feel was mismanaging funds that were for that part of the business.

Q. Anything else?

A. That's all I can think of at this time.

Q. So you've now told me everything you believe G did which constitutes mismanaging the business?

A. At this moment that's all I can think of.

Q. Do you believe a partner in a partnership has a right to terminate the partnership? Any partner in any partnership. Has nothing to do with "My Business". I'm just asking for your understanding. And if you don't know, you don't know.

ATTORNEY 1: Objection, iGroper hypothetical.

ATTORNEY 2: Let me finish the question.

ATTORNEY 1: Sorry, I apologize.

Q. (By ATTORNEY 2) Do you believe that a partner in a partnership has a right to terminate the partnership?

A. Yes.

ATTORNEY 1: Objection.

Q. (By ATTORNEY 2) Okay. Thank you. Do you believe that G breached the agreement between the two of you?

A. The partnership agreement?

Q. Yes.

A. Yes, I do.

Q. Before you tell me, I'm going to ask you what constitutes a breach. What persons other than you have knowledge of any of the acts which you believe constitute breaches?

A. Bank account.

Q. That's not a person.

ATTORNEY 1: That's a legal person actually.

THE WITNESS: Okay.

Q. (By ATTORNEY 2) Is there someone at Bank account that you know?
A. I don't specifically know a certain person, but when G cancelled my debit card, she did not have permission to do that, and the Bank admitted that they were in wrong for eliminating my access via my debit card to that account.
Q. Maybe it's easier to do it the other way.
  Why don't you enumerate for me all of the acts or conduct which you believe constitute breaches of contract, and then we'll go back to who has knowledge of those acts.

So tell me what you believe constitutes a breach of contract?
ATTORNEY 1: Objection, calls for a legal conclusion and also calls for a narrative. Maybe you can be more specific with your question and tailor it to this M.er and not -
ATTORNEY 2: Go ahead and answer, please.
ATTORNEY 1: – what across the board is -
ATTORNEY 2: You've made your objection.

Q. Go ahead and answer.
A. Could you please reread that question.
Q. Do you agree that it's your assertion that G breached the contract between the two of you?
A. I believe that G has –
Q. Yes or no.
A. – violated the partnership agreement between us, yes.
Q. Tell me all the things which you believe constitute violation of the partnership agreement.
A. Withdrawing money without permission of the partnership. Closing the business without agreement of the partnership. Changing the passwords without agreement of the partnership. Posting the **** that was not approved by me as a violation of the agreement.
Taking funds.
That's all I can think of at this moment.
Q. Okay. Now, as to – let's take them individually. You've identified four things: Withdrawing money, closing the business, changing passwords and posting the *****. So as to withdrawing money, who has knowledge of that fact or circumstance besides you and G? The answer may be no one.
A. I would say the Bank account. I don't know that anybody else knows that.

Q. Okay. Who has knowledge of G closing the business other than you and G?   ATTORNEY 1: Objection.
THE WITNESS: Oh, that's a big question. That's a big one.
Q. (By ATTORNEY 2) That's fine. Tell me as many people as you want.
A. I don't know –
ATTORNEY 1: This is duplicative information that's contained in the coGlaint and the discovery responses that we've provided to you earlier. I really think this isn't advancing the ball at all to rehash this. Maybe make her –
ATTORNEY 2: Make an objection.
ATTORNEY 1: – read off of the documents and ask her anything in addition to those things?
I'm objecting. As I said, it's duplicative.
ATTORNEY 2: Fine. You've made your objection.
Q. Answer the question.
A. So everyone that has gone back to the website to take a course would know that the business is closed. Most of the co-workers at work know that the business is closed because they've tried to take ****.
Q. Okay.
A. G sent out an email stating G was closing the business, so all of our customers know that the business is closed. Our vendors, actually I don't know that they know –
Q. Let me word it a little differently.
A. – if the business is closed.
ATTORNEY 1: Attorney 2, she was still answering. So perhaps you could allow her to coGletely finish her answer.
Q. (By ATTORNEY 2) Anything else you wanted to tell me about?

ATTORNEY 1: Go ahead, H.
THE WITNESS: I've lost my train thought.

> ***When you are over five hours into this process, and the room feels like 90 degrees it is miserable.

Q. (By ATTORNEY 2) So let me ask it a little differently. Is there anyone else who you believe has knowledge of your allegation that H closed the business improperly?
A. I never closed the business.

> ***He was sly on his questioning. I don't know if he did this on purpose, or if it was truly a mistake. I was happy that I caught this one. I began to wonder if he asked certain questions to see if I was still paying attention.

Q. I'm sorry, that G closed the business iGroperly?
ATTORNEY 1: Objection, calls for a – calls for facts that are not in the evidence that the business is actually closed. And objection as to vague and ambiguous as to what is meant by closed. Are we talking about the partnership or the online company sites that people can – if you can provide explanation as to that, she might have a better time of answering. ATTORNEY 2: Now he's finished. Now you get to talk.
Q. What's your answer?
A. Could you please repeat the question.
Q. Sure. You have said that one of the breaches of contract was closing the business, right?
A. Correct.

Q. So what I'm asking you is, who other than you has knowledge of the facts by which you allege that G closing the business was a breach of contract?
A. My husband.
Q. Okay.
A. I don't – I'm just going to say my husband.
Q. Who other than you and G has knowledge that G changed the passwords other than the vendors who deal with the passwords? Anyone else you're aware of?
A. My husband.
Q. Okay.
A. And my attorneys.
Q. And same question, who has knowledge of the posting of the ***** other than the two of you?

ATTORNEY 1: Objection. What posting of -objection as vague and ambiguous as to what posting of what *****. Are we talking – at what time? What year? The last posting? The dispute regarding the posting? Could you please provide clarification so she can answer it specifically.

ATTORNEY 2: Go ahead and answer.

ATTORNEY 1: If you want clarification from him, you can ask for it. You're not required to respond to a question you don't understand.

THE WITNESS: Could you please repeat the question.

Q. (By ATTORNEY 2) Sure. You gave me four alleged breaches of contract. The fourth one in your words were posting courses without my permission, okay. And I'm asking you, who has knowledge of the facts and circumstances of that allegation that she posted courses without your permission other than the two of you?
A. My husband.

Q. Anyone else?

A. Not that I can recall at this time.

Q. So as you proceed toward trial, do you know of anyone else that you would call as a witness to support any of your allegations regarding breaches of contract other than perhaps you and your husband?

A. Could I please revisit my answers now that –

Q. We've moved on.

A. I may have answered them –
ATTORNEY 1: She's speaking right now.
THE WITNESS: But I may have answered those wrong, and – okay, could you repeat your question.

> ***Now I was starting to worry over what I was being asked, and if how I was answering was correct.

Q. (By ATTORNEY 2) Sure. What I'm asking you now is, who do you anticipate calling as a witness at trial to testify to having personal knowledge of these alleged breaches of contract which you've just described?
ATTORNEY 1: Objection, calls for potentially attorney/client privileged communication. To the extent that it's not – it's independent, feel free to disclose that information.
THE WITNESS: Feel free to answer the question?
ATTORNEY 1: Yes. So anything that was specifically only discussed in attorney/client communications -
THE WITNESS: So only answer -
ATTORNEY 2: I'm not asking ever about anything you ever discussed with your attorneys. ATTORNEY 1: I'm doing that for her clarification because it's so easy to –

My Crazy Deposition

Q. (By ATTORNEY 2) We're a week from trial. You know who your witnesses are. I'm just asking that. Who are they?

> ***We were less than a week from trial, and my firm had not talked to me about who they were going to call from the list of people I had provided. I would have thought they would have called them all, but they had not subpoenaed anyone on my list.

A. That's a discussion between me and my attorney.
ATTORNEY 1: Oh, yeah.

Q. (By ATTORNEY 2) But you have the knowledge in your head separate and apart from what you've discussed. I'm not asking you to just tell me what the two of you discussed. I'm asking your knowledge of people. Who are the people who had knowledge? Who are the people you would ask to support your testimony?
ATTORNEY 1: May I clarify for her a little?
ATTORNEY 2: No. You can object to the question. That's all.
ATTORNEY 1: I'm trying to be helpful, Attorney B.
THE WITNESS: I don't think there's anybody different than who's been put on the forms that I had filled out.

Q. (By ATTORNEY 2) There is no forms that have been filled out in front of us.
ATTORNEY 1: Objection, argumentative.

Q. (By ATTORNEY 2) I'm asking today who these people are. You may have changed your mind since then. You may never have put anyone down. I don't know who you think you put down. I'm asking you today, one week before trial, who do you think can testify to the support of the things you have told us? Don't testify for her. Go ahead.

ATTORNEY 1: Wow, you're a nice guy.

THE WITNESS: I believe that the people I have addressed on the forms would be the only people that would –

Q. (By ATTORNEY 2) And who are those people?

A. I can't remember who all I have put on those forms.

Q. I'm entitled to your recollection without regard to what you put on forms. Tell me what you know today as you sit here.

ATTORNEY 1: Objection, asked and answered. She says she does not recall. You might not like –

Q. (By ATTORNEY 2) Is that your answer?

ATTORNEY 1: If you recall, you may tell him any –

Q. (By ATTORNEY 2) If you want to tell me that's your answer, that's fine.

A. That's my answer.

Q. So you sit here ten days, a week before trial, and you don't recall a single person who has knowledge that you would call to testify in support of your allegations? Is that what you're telling me?

ATTORNEY 1: Objection, asked and answered. She's already answered this, Attorney 2. She's answered this -

THE WITNESS: Correct.

ATTORNEY 1: – twice now. This would be the third time.

ATTORNEY 2: Okay. Thank you.

Q. Can you identify anything you believe G ever put online which was **** from another person?

A. The ******** for sure.

Q. Anything else?

A. That's the only ones that I know of to date.

Q. And in your mind, are ******************* the same?

ATTORNEY 1: Objection. That's calling for her to reach legal conclusions that she's not qualified to make.

THE WITNESS: I don't think they're the same. I think they're different. I believe using ************ is different than using **********, and I know that ********** –

Q. (By ATTORNEY 2) Okay. I asked the question because the coGlaint separately alleges that G ****** on others' **********. So you have alleged both *****************. Is it your understanding that that which was*******************? . . . .**************?

A. The ******************.

Q. And you're not aware of anything other than those ********************?

A. I'm not aware of anything other than those ********************.

Q. Do you believe the business was devalued in some way because those ****** were posted?

A. I believe those ****** set us up for possible lawsuits for********************.

Q. Do you believe that the business was devalued because of that?

ATTORNEY 1: Objection. You've asked that, and she's answered that.

THE WITNESS: I believe the bigger concern was *************************.

Q. (By ATTORNEY 2) I understand you –

A. And it looked bad.

Q. – said that.

A. I do believe it devalued it in the fact that it *************.
Q. By how much did it devalue it?
A. I cannot estimate it –
ATTORNEY 1: Actually calls for –
(Reporter interruption.)

> ***I cannot say what the reporter was thinking. I do know she said this had to stop. She talked for a few minutes this time. Attorney 2 was talking very fast, and she was frustrated with this.

Q. (By ATTORNEY 2) Do you know how much? And your answer was, I don't know?   ATTORNEY 1: I would like to make my objection. That calls for a legal conclusion.
THE WITNESS: And I don't know.
Q. (By ATTORNEY 2) What do you think the business is worth today?
ATTORNEY 1: Objection, calls for a legal conclusion and potentially -
ATTORNEY 2: If you want to tell me she's -
ATTORNEY 1: Can I finish my objection, Attorney 2. Please, I was speaking. I still was speaking. You can speak after and tell me what a terrible person I am and everything else, and that's fine. And you don't like me, and I'm not as smart as you. That's cool. But I want to make my objection, okay. I want to preserve on the record my objection, whether you agree with it or disagree with it. Can I just finish, okay?
I'm really trying not to interrupt you, and I've made that effort since about an hour and a half into this deposition. So my objection was it calls for a legal conclusion and

potentially calls for attorney/client privileged communication. To the extent that, of course, you can answer without going into that, feel free to.

ATTORNEY 2: If you're going to tell me she's not going to testify to it at trial, then I won't ask the questions.

ATTORNEY 1: I didn't say that.

ATTORNEY 2: But if you don't tell me that, then you can't object.

ATTORNEY 1: Oh, yes, I can object. My objection stands.

Q. (By ATTORNEY 2) What do you understand today to be the value of the business, "My Business" business?

A. I do not have at this moment an evaluation of the business.

Q. Are you going to testify to it at trial? Because I'm entitled to know. Because if you don't tell me today, I'm going to ask that a court not let you testify to it. So I'm giving you that warning. You can't tell me today "I don't know," and then come in a week from now and say "I now know."

So are you going to testify or do you believe you're going to testify to what the value of the business is?

ATTORNEY 1: Objection. This is argumentative. You're giving her false alternatives and telling her this is the only option.

ATTORNEY 2: So make an objection.

ATTORNEY 1: She can say "I don't recall" rather than "I don't know," and she can still viably go and present testimony at trial of it.

ATTORNEY 2: So make an objection if you have one.

ATTORNEY 1: I did. I did.

Q. (By ATTORNEY 2) What do you believe to be the value of the business today?

A. I do not know.

Q. What do you believe to be the – to have been the value of the business January 1st, 2015? ATTORNEY 1: May I have a moment with my client, Attorney 2?
ATTORNEY 2: No.
ATTORNEY 1: I would like to take a break.

> ***The heat was unbearable. I needed a drink of water, and I needed out of the heat. I was getting so hot I was having a hard time thinking.

ATTORNEY 2: She can answer the question, and then you can talk all you want. There's a question pending.
THE WITNESS: January 1st, the business was not evaluated. So I do not know at that time how much the business was worth.

Q. (By ATTORNEY 2) I'm not asking whether it was valued by a third party. You had an opinion on January 1st, 2015. So I'm asking what your opinion was of the value of the business January 1st, 2015.
ATTORNEY 1: Objection, assuming facts not in evidence. She never said that she had an opinion in January 1st, 2015, or whatever the date was, of the value of the partnership. I recall nothing being ever – she's never said that. So if you're asking her if at that time she had that, please ask it in that form, but -
ATTORNEY 2: Again you get to answer my questions, not his.

Q. What was your opinion of the value of the business January 1, 2015?

A. I was not thinking about the value of the business on January 1st, 2015.

Q. So is your answer "I don't know"?
A. No.
Q. Okay. Then what is your answer?
A. I can tell you that on January 1st, I was not thinking about the value of the business.
Q. What do you believe today was the value of the business on January 1st, 2015?
A. I do not know.
Q. Have you made any effort to learn what it was then or what it is now?
A. Not on January 1st –
ATTORNEY 1: Objection – sorry. I'd like to make the objection.
THE WITNESS: Go ahead.
ATTORNEY 1: It calls for potentially attorney/client privileged communication. To the extent you can answer without breaching that, answer. Or if you don't recall or you don't know, you can say that as well.
THE WITNESS: Could you please repeat the question.
Q. (By ATTORNEY 2) What do you understand today -well, strike that. Go ahead and repeat it. That's a better record of exactly what I said. (Whereupon the question "Have you made any effort to learn what it was then or what it is now" was read back as requested.)
THE WITNESS: I have not made any effort to find out what the business was worth January 1st, 2015.
Q. (By ATTORNEY 2) Same answer for today? Have you made any effort to find out what it's worth today?
ATTORNEY 1: Objection – sorry, go ahead. It was a compound question, but he's broken it down, so you can answer.

THE WITNESS: I have not hired anyone to evaluate the business for what the value is at this time. I am sorry. I am dying of heat. Can I step out again?

***The heat was really getting to me at this point. I was so dry I felt like I could barely talk and I needed to drink some water.

ATTORNEY 2: Sure. We're almost done.
(Recess taken from 3:23 p.m. to 3:33 p.m.)

***There is still almost an hour worth of questions, and It was just getting to be too much.

Q. (By ATTORNEY 2) Let me go back for a minute and talk about your comments that one of the breaches of the partnership agreement was purportedly G's acts in putting ****** that we've been talking about in February of 2015. What was the name of that ****** by the way?
A. *********.
Q. Your comment was G put that course online before giving you an opportunity to **** it, right?
A. Correct.
Q. Did you ever **** any of the other ****** G wrote –
A. Can I change my answer to that?
Q. Sure.
A. The opportunity to look at it and approve it, not so much *** it. But I was supposed to be able to approve that ****.
Q. Okay. Did you approve every other ****** ***** wrote before it went online?
A. No.

My Crazy Deposition

Q. So what was different this time?

A. Because of our disagreement over the ******, the agreement from there on was that each one of us was supposed to be able to see each other's ***** and make an approval on whether or not it could be posted or not.

Q. When you say the agreement was, what exactly do you mean?

A. The agreement was each one of us was to be able to look at each other's ****************.

Q. So when you say an agreement, I'm assuming you don't mean anything formal in writing? You're just talking about an oral understanding between the two of you?

A. Correct. And it's actually documented in an email.

Q. Is it your understanding that C was ***** all of G's ****** as well as yours?

A. Correct.

Q. Is it your understanding that anybody else had ever ****** any of G's ******?

A. I had no idea that anybody else would be editing G's ******.

Q. So it was your belief right up to the end that C saw everything, and you don't know if anyone else was seeing anything?

ATTORNEY 1: Objection, vague and ambiguous as to everything. Are you talking about G's courses or G and H's courses still?

ATTORNEY 2: Both.

THE WITNESS: For my *******, I was under the understanding that C was looking at them up to the point of the*********.

Q. (By ATTORNEY 2) Okay.
A. I'm sorry. I'd like to change that answer. I'd like to change that answer. Up to the w c. Because after the *******, ** was *** my ******.
Q. Didn't ** only edit like one course?
A. No. She did the ******* and the *******.
Q. And didn't *** do such an atrocious job that you agreed just to go back and have C do it?
A. I thought *** did a great job, and I thought we worked very well, and I never agreed to go back to –
Q. ** is the ************* you found? Is that –
A. She's actually a English major that has graduated with an English degree and has ****** for the R C.
Q. But at the time **** was in college, right?
A. *** was in *** final year of college.
Q. All right. Do you believe you have sustained some monetary loss as a result of any of the allegations of my client which brings us here today?
A. Yes.
Q. Okay. What loss?
A. I believe there are loss from the work that I have done. I believe there's a loss of future income. I believe there was a loss of possible income while G was in control of the business because there was no growth that I was aware of because I was locked out of the Vendor to verify what was or what was not going on at that time. And the loss from G not continuing the Marketing advertising.

> ***I should have added closing the business. This was addressed in court, and there was a claim that the amount of clients went up, but that

number was never produced in interrogatories or court.

Q. Isn't that the same as the other categories?
Because you said future income. Isn't that –
A. I believe they're different categories all contributing to the different losses.
Q. They're all contributing to a monetary future loss, right?
ATTORNEY 1: I'm sorry –
THE WITNESS: No. I think that some were for –

> ***I should have finished my thought.

ATTORNEY 2: Okay. We'll explore them separately.
Q. You've started by – the first category of damages is, from the work I've done. What does that mean?

> ***I missed that he changed the word from loss to damages, and I am not sure at the time I caught the change because I continue to use the word loss.

A. The hours that I've invested in this company. With the business now being closed, I feel that that work has been lost.
Q. Why is it lost?
Don't you still have what you wrote?
A. No.
Q. What do you mean, no?
You don't have the ****** you wrote somewhere on your Computer at home?
A. But I don't have control of those *******.

Q. Why not?

A. Because we have not settled the dispute between – of the business. I –

Q. What is – I'm sorry, go ahead and finish.

A. I don't feel that we've addressed all aspects of this business appropriately. And until that's done, I will not do anything with any parts of this business. It's still to remain whole until it's completed throughout this process.

Q. Don't you believe you own what you wrote?

A. I absolutely believe I own what I wrote.

Q. So don't you believe you can sell what you wrote to someone else if you want, for example?

A. I believe that would be conflict until this dispute has been settled in court.

Q. What is the future income you believe you've lost? Characterize, and then I'm going to ask the same question in dollars. So what do you believe in words is the future income you've lost?

A. I'm sorry. With your discussion, I kind of lost what you were asking.

Q. I'm asking you to describe it, and then I'm going to ask what the monetary value of it is. So first what are you characterizing or describing as future income?

A. That would have been from the time if the business was still being – was being advertised and was still having the – between the 50 and the nine and the 73 percent growth that we had established over those years, I believe that would be the future loss that this company has.

> ***I must have lost my train of thought. On average the business was growing 63%, and one

My Crazy Deposition

of the most recent years had a 73% growth. The business was growing.

Q. So you're talking future income to have been derived from the operations of "My Business"?
A. Correct, based on the past history of the –
Q. And what do you believe that future income would have been?
A. I don't have those numbers in front of me.
Q. Well, again you have to testify to them in seven or eight days.
A. So I do not recall those numbers at this time.
Q. Do you have them somewhere?
A. Not on me, sir, I do not.
Q. Does someone have these numbers?
A. I believe that's client privileged information at this time.
Q. Well, you have not disclosed any accounting witnesses to testify to this, so you're the only one who gets to. So what do you believe the loss to be? And if you don't know exactly –
A. I do not recall those numbers at this time.
Q. What's your best estimate?
A. I do not have an estimate at this time.
Q. So you have no estimate whatsoever as you sit here today of what the loss you sustained is?   Again you've got to stop looking at him and answer my questions.
ATTORNEY 1: I might be able to assist her a minute.
ATTORNEY 2: You don't get to testify. If you have an objection to my question, make it. ATTORNEY 1: Attorney 2, I get that. I'm trying to facilitate an answer for you that will be helpful and you won't be upset about everything at the end of the day.

ATTORNEY 2: I don't want you giving her the answer though.
ATTORNEY 1: I'm not giving her the answer. I'm going to perhaps help her – okay.
THE WITNESS: I do not know those figures at this moment.

> ***This was extremely hard because there were different categories, and there were different totals for different categories for each year. None of those had been brought together by attorneys at that time. I did not want to give the wrong amounts and be held to them. I did not want to give too low of an amount.

Q. (By ATTORNEY 2) What's your best estimate of those figures?
A. I do not recall the numbers that I – I do not recall the numbers at this time.
Q. Is it more than a dollar?
A. Yes.
Q. Is it more than a hundred dollars?
A. Yes.
Q. Over how many years do you believe you can carry out losses? One year? Two years? Five years? A hundred years?
ATTORNEY 1: Objection, calls for a legal conclusion.
Q. (By ATTORNEY 2) You still get to answer.

ATTORNEY 1: Do you even understand the question?

THE WITNESS: I do understand the question. I do not know – I do not have those figures or those thoughts that has been discussed between my attorney and I at this time.

> ***I had run those figures based on current gross income, and every year until I was to retired, just out of curiosity. I knew the plan was to only ask a couple of years, but the attorneys had not set the exact amount at that time. I did not want to guess or estimate.

Q. (By ATTORNEY 2) That question doesn't ask for any figures. I'm asking for your understanding of how many years you can ask for damages. One year? Two years? Five years? A hundred years?
A. I don't recall.
Q. Are your losses more than a million dollars?
A. No.
Q. Are your losses more than five hundred thousand?
A. I don't recall the figures at this time.
Q. Your total combined monetary losses that you're going to ask a judge to award you in a few days, do you understand that number to exceed five hundred thousand dollars?
A. I do not recall those numbers at this time.
Q. Do you believe – you've told me it's not a million?
A. It's not a million.

> ***No, the losses were not going to be over five hundred thousand, but I did not want to commit. I understood why he was doing this, but it was very frustrating when you are sitting there. He was being condescending.

Q. Is it more than nine hundred fifty thousand?
A. I do not recall those numbers at this time.
Q. So it might be nine hundred fifty thousand?
A. I don't know those numbers at this time.
Q. You don't have any idea other than it's less than a million dollars and more than a dollar?
Is that what you're telling me?
ATTORNEY 1: Objection. That's mischaracterizing what she's testified. She siGly responded to your questions on those -
ATTORNEY 2: Make an objection.
ATTORNEY 1: I did. You're mischaracterizing -
ATTORNEY 2: That's not an objection.
ATTORNEY 1: – her testimony.
THE WITNESS: I do not recall the numbers that you are asking me for.
Q. (By ATTORNEY 2) So all you are comfortable answering today is that you believe your losses are more than a dollar and less than a million dollars?
ATTORNEY 1: Objection. You're mischaracterizing her prior statements.
Q. (By ATTORNEY 2) Is that correct?
A. Could you please repeat the question.
Q. Are you telling me that all you know as you sit here right now is that you believe your damages to be more than a dollar and less than a million dollars?
A. I do not recall those numbers at this time.
Q. I'm not asking you any numbers.
I'm asking, is it your belief that your damages are more than a dollar but less than a million dollars?
A. I do not recall.

My Crazy Deposition

Q. So your damages might be more than a million?
A. I answered that question to say no.
Q. Well, then less than a million, right? Then why would you not agree they're less than a million? You've said they're not more than a million, but you won't say it's less than a million. I don't understand that.
A. I may have misunderstood the question that you asked me. So could you please repeat the question.

> ***He acted as if he was very upset, and the questions were being asked quickly. At some point I felt I needed to stick to one answer. I was trying to slow things down, especially since my attorney was trying to be a part of this discussion.

Q. Sure. Do you agree that as you sit here today you are not able to tell me anything more about your damages other than that they are more than one dollar and less than one million dollars? ATTORNEY 1: Objection. Again you're mischaracterizing prior statements of the witness.
Q. (By ATTORNEY 2) Is that correct?
A. I do not recall the numbers that –
Q. Again I am not –
A. I understand you're not asking me for a number, but I do not recall. I do not recall. ATTORNEY 1: Objection. This has been asked and answered multiple times. And she's given an answer, and you don't like the answer. I get that, Attorney 2. However, she has given an answer. And if you want to continue to narrow it down, you're asking range questions, and that could – it seems to be compound in a

sense. So maybe you could try a different approach rather than the current approach.

ATTORNEY 2: Are you done yet?

ATTORNEY 1: Yes, sir.

ATTORNEY 2: Thank you.

Q. You're telling me you don't know what your damages are. I'm past that, okay. I'm not asking you what your damages are. I'm asking you to confirm that you have no knowledge of what your damages are as you sit here today. So can you confirm that you do not know what your damages are other than to say that they're more than a dollar and less than a million dollars? That's one you can't say "I don't know" to.

ATTORNEY 1: Actually, sir, you're harassing.

Q. (By ATTORNEY 2) You either confirm it or you don't.

ATTORNEY 1: Sir, you're harassing her. You're harassing her. You're being -

THE WITNESS: I feel like I've answered the question.

ATTORNEY 1: – argumentative, and I'm objecting to that.

THE WITNESS: So at this time I do not recall.

Q. (By ATTORNEY 2) Okay. I am asking you to confirm as true or false, okay. So you can't not answer. You can't say "I don't know."· It is a statement that is either true or it is false. I don't care what the answer is. I just want to know what the answer is. True or false, as you sit here at this moment, you do not know what your damages are other than that they're more than a dollar and less than a million dollars? True or false. True or false that you do not know?

ATTORNEY 1: Objection to your compound question and requiring her to only answer one of two answers.

It's again an informal fallacy of the alternative option. I'm sorry, you can answer more than true or false to that question if you want.

THE WITNESS: I do not recall.

Q. (By ATTORNEY 2) I'm going to ask your lawyer – and he doesn't have to agree – to go out and take a break and talk to you. Because I will tell you right now, if you do not answer my questions, I will file a motion before the court to preclude you from telling me in any respect what your damages are, because I'm entitled to that information. And he could have disclosed some other witness that was going to provide that information, and then I would have been duty-bound to ask the person, but he did not. So you are the only witness who can testify to damages. And if you are now telling me that you do not know what your damages are and cannot testify to it, I will ask the court to prevent you from testifying to it. So if you want to go talk about it and come back in and answer those questions, great. If you want to continue where you are today, that's fine. I have no problem with that. But I will ask the court to prevent you from providing any evidence of damage.

A. So I would like to step out and talk –

ATTORNEY 1: Yeah, we'll go off the record.

Thank you.

(Recess taken at 3:47 p.m. to 3:54 p.m.)

> ***I had no Idea if what he was saying was true or not. I did not have exact figures, and I did not want to give too low of a figure. I did want an opportunity to speak to my attorney before committing to any figures, and I was happy to

have this opportunity. Going back in, I gave a high range to leave myself room. My Attorney told me they still had not decided how to address the figures, and what the figures were going to be.

Q. (By ATTORNEY 2) Ms., now that we took a break and you've had an opportunity to speak with your counsel, do you want to revisit the damage issues and tell me what you think you've lost in this M.er?
A. So we're asking for – could you please repeat the question.
Q. Well, the question is simply, do you want to change any of your answers and address the question of damages? If the answer is no, I'll move on. If the answer is yes, I'll ask questions again.
A. So is this where I'm giving you a range? I don't understand the question.
Q. I'm asking you a yes or no question. Do you want to say something else –
A. Could you please repeat the question.
Q. The question is, now that you've had a chance to talk to your lawyer, do you want to revisit the issue of damages and provide additional information?
A. Yes, sir.
Q. What do you believe you've said before that you'd like to change?
A. Can I say that – I'm sorry.
Oh, the range.
Q. Okay. What is that?
A. Between *** and *** thousand.
Q. How do you compute a low end range of *** dollars?

A. I do not recall the breakdown.
Q. So you just all of a sudden went out in the hallway and remember a number, but you don't have any idea how you came to that number?
Is that what you're telling me?
A. I'm giving you the best estimate that I can give you without having the actual paperwork in front of me.
Q. What are the components of that *** dollars?
A. The loss of future income, the cost of what it would be to re- -- to get the business back up and running where it was to the point that it was shut down. Hours that were put into this business. I do not recall all the components of how we came to those figures.
Q. What are those numbers on an annual basis?
A. I'm not sure I understand the question.

> ***How my attorneys were addressing the figures, and how he was asking the questions did not fall into the same categories. The figures my attorneys were working on did not all fall into an annual basis so I was unable to answer the question. It was like comparing apples to oranges. My case did not fit into one box, there were several small ones.

Q. Okay. In other words, I don't know whether you're saying, I would have had one more year in this business and I would have made three hundred thousand in this year, so two fifty to four is reasonable. Or are you saying, I would have made 20,000 a year for ten years, and that's how you come to a minimum of *** hundred something?

So I need to know how many years you're estimating in that analysis so I can figure out what you're deeming to be an annual breakdown.

A. I do not recall the specific number, but I'm going to estimate it out to be two.

Q. So you're telling me in two years you would have earned between *** and ***?

A. No, sir. What I'm saying is, I do not recall the components that we used to come to that calculation, and that I'm basing the future – loss of future income off of two years, the costs that it would entail to be able to bring the business back up to where it's at today within those two years, and the damages of what I've put into this business in hours and have lost because the business was closed.

Q. Okay. So I think we're saying the same thing.

***We were not "saying the same thing". Again, his words.

You're telling me that you would have lost *** to **** dollars over the course of two years?

A. I'm not saying lost. I'm saying to bring the business back up to where it was the day that it was closed. There's also a cost to that.

Q. And that's included in the two *** to **** hundred?

A. But I'm not sure how we broke that out.

Q. Again let me go back to – I'm trying to understand. When one presents loss of damage calculations, it's based on an annualized loss to the business. If the business loses 50,000 dollars a year, in five years I've lost 250,000 dollars. You've given me the numbers. I'm trying to understand how many years it took you to get to that number. So how

many years do you think it would have taken for you to have lost ***** dollars?
ATTORNEY 1: Objection. It's vague and ambiguous as to what damages we're actually talking about and what components, and I think it's creating confusion in Ms. 's response.

> ***My attorneys had given me several different ways that they planned to approach this, and each way had a different amount. They had not decided which direction they wanted to approach damages. I was unable to give an answer to a question my attorney did not have an answer to. I was in between a rock, and a hard place.

ATTORNEY 2: Again you're now testifying. That's not an objection.
THE WITNESS: I understand that, sir. So what I'm telling you is that I cannot recall how it was broken down, those exact numbers of how it was broken down, and that not all of those figures were based on losses, because you're addressing the losses. Some of those figures were addressing bringing the business back to the point it would be – it would need to be back where it is in two years.

Q. (By ATTORNEY 2) What do you understand G did when G closed the business?
ATTORNEY 1: Objection, calls for speculation. To the point you do understand, you may testify. THE WITNESS: I'm sorry, sir, could you please repeat the question.

Q. (By ATTORNEY 2) What do you understand G did to close the business?
ATTORNEY 1: Also objection as to -
THE WITNESS: G pulled the business off the Internet.
Q. (By ATTORNEY 2) Okay. Anything else?
A. I have no idea what else was done to the business because I still do not have access to all components of the business.
Q. So if G shut down the website, so to speak –
A. Uh-huh.

> ***I was getting tired at this point, and I was physically and emotionally worn down.

Q. – what do you understand is necessary to turn the website back on?
A. If I was to turn back on the business, I would have to apply to the *** with no guarantees that I would be able to start that business up again. That would have to be based on the approval of whether or not the *** would allow me to start that business back up. And then to get the business back where it was today, I would have to reinvest all that time and money to get it back to the spot that it was at today.
Q. What do you believe it would cost to do that? A range.
A. Could you clarify that question, please.
Q. Yeah. You've just told me what happened and what you believe you would have to do to start it again. I'm asking you what you think it would cost.
A. I do not recall the figures that we have been working on.
Q. In fact can it be done in an hour?
You just reactivate the website, and you're done?
A. No, sir.

Q. Why not?
A. Because I –
ATTORNEY 1: Objection.
Q. (By ATTORNEY 2) You may not know, but if you do, tell me why not.
ATTORNEY 1: Okay. I'm objecting because it does call for a potential disclosure of some attorney/client privileged communication.

And to the extent you can answer, answer. But to the extent you can't, I'm advising you not to.
Q. (By ATTORNEY 2) The question is, why not?
A. I can't just turn it on until – like I said before, I would have to reapply to the *** to make sure that I got approval to restart the business in my name only.
Q. I'm not talking about your name only. I'm just talking about a business. There is a business that was "My Business" that was closed by someone turning off the website. To your knowledge, is there any reason why the website can't be reactivated today, for example?
A. I have not communicated with M. to see if that is still available to me. I don't know what components of that part of the business are still there, not there. I have no idea what's happened to that.

> ***As far as I knew, once G shut down the business everything was lost, and had to be re-recreated. It was not as easy as flipping on a switch, and having everything right there available. This company, if re-opened, would have to be restarted from the ground up just like it was from day one. Nothing was there to

> just start from, there was a lot more to this. In court attorney 2 kept saying it just a matter of flipping a switch and turning it back on.

Q. So is the –
A. I do not know for the Vendor. Just because we reactivate that business does not mean that those customers are still going to come back.

> ***This was true. Not every client goes back to a business that all of a sudden closed its doors. In fact, most customers will not go back to a company who makes promises, and then does not keep them. In some cases it is better to just start from scratch.

Q. I understand that. I'm not asking you that.
A. So the business isn't going to be the same business if you just turn it back on.
Q. Are you aware of any reason why you cannot just turn the website back on?
A. The *** clearly states that I would need to reapply and be approved before I could turn that business back on.
Q. Aren't you presupposing in that answer that the business has a different owner?
A. The *** clearly states that if there are any changes to a business, it must be reported. And the *** may not approve that business being run at that time by me. I don't know that, but -Q.   So you're –
A. – I would have to apply to the *** to see if I was approved.
Q. You're answering different questions. You're answering as presupposing you started the business. I'm not presuppos-

ing you personally start the business. I'm just talking the business. There was a business that existed. Its website was turned off. I'm just asking, is there any reason why that website for that same "My Business" business without regard to who owned it could be turned back on?

> ***I was not answering a different question, I was not giving him the answer he wanted. He kept asking the same questions until I messed up, and gave him the answer he wanted. Then, he used them against me in court.

ATTORNEY 1: Objection. I think she has answered this previously.
ATTORNEY 2: Trust me, she hasn't.
ATTORNEY 1: I'm not going to trust you, and my objection stands. So objection, asked and answered.
THE WITNESS: I do not have any idea if that business could be just turned back on.
ATTORNEY 2: Thank you.

Q. What damages do you attribute to what you described as the Marketing problem?
A. There was a loss of customers coming in.
Q. Identify for me if you can any of the customers you think you lost because of Marketing.
A. Our business is set up to where we would never know whether those customers came up.
Q. So you don't know how many of them, if any, were lost, do you?
A. I can state that there are click throughs from
   Marketing to – that matched almost exactly to the *****
   that have logged on to Vendor, so I think it's reasonable

to not assume but to – to feel that at least a percentage of those that have clicked through are customers from Marketing.

Q. Do you have any knowledge of how many customers the business had December 31st, 2014?

A. I don't know of that –

ATTORNEY 1: Asked and answered and -

THE WITNESS: – particular day, but I do have a log.

My Crazy Deposition

Q. (By ATTORNEY 2) Approximately. I'm just asking about the end of the year.
A. There was a guesstimate. Not an exact number. Would have been somewhere around twenty-seven-hundred-and-some customers.
Q. Is that people who have taken tests? Is that how you're defining customers?
A. I would have to go back and look at the information. So I do not recall that information.
Q. But when you use the word **** – I'm sorry. When you use the word "customers," you're talking about people who have taken *****?
A. I'm talking about the amount of users that we have.
Q. What's a user?
A. A user is a person that is logged into our company and has at least looked at the courses to see if there is a course they were going to take.
Q. So a user or a customer may not be someone who ever took a ****? It's someone who logged in at the website?
A. What I would do once a year is go through the list and clear that list out, or if there were multiple log-ons –
Q. You're beating around the bush.

> ***Here is another comment to get me angry because he is not getting the answers he wants.

A. Could I please finish my answer. You asked me a question, and I'm trying to answer the question that I feel you've asked.
Q. Fine, but you're not even close.
A. So I would like to finish this –

Q. Go ahead.
   ATTORNEY 2: Object. Attorney 2 –
   THE WITNESS: Would you like –
   (Reporter interruption.)
   (Discussion was held off the record.)

   >***The recorder was doing the best she could in this chaos, I feel at this point she was getting tired of this deposition as well. It was getting to the point of ridiculous, this constant attacking. He is definitely good at his job, and he knows how to throw someone off their train of thought. He must have been getting ready to throw me another curve ball. I did appreciate the recorder stopping, and intervening at this time. It helped to slow the questions down.

Q. (By ATTORNEY 2) Ms., you're well past my question. I don't care about any of that information. That's not what I'm asking at the moment. Let me just ask the yes-or-no question I've tried to ask. You used the word "customers.". You talked about a customer as someone who logged on to the website. All I'm asking is, is that different than people who took the ***? Is that the same, or is it different?

   >***My point exactly. If he didn't care about any of the information, then why was he asking it? I felt he was using it to slide in a different wording, and with the speed being slowed down that opportunity was lost.

   ATTORNEY 1: Do you understand the question?

My Crazy Deposition

THE WITNESS: I don't have enough information at this time to answer that question correctly. ATTORNEY 2: Fine. That's all I'm asking.

Q. Do you have any idea how many customers, however you define a customer, the company had December 31st, 2015?
A. No, I do not.

> ***I knew approximately how much was made in those years, but not the exact amount down to the penny. I was instructed unless I remembered the exact number, not to guess.

Q. Do you know what the gross revenues were in 2015 compared to 2014?
A. I do not remember the – I do not recall the specific numbers of those – of those years at this time.
Q. Do you know how many tests were taken in 2015 compared to 2014?
A. No, I do not, because I was logged out of the website.
Q. So if you were to learn that there were more tests taken and more revenues generated, would you still think the business went down in value in 2015?
A. Yes.

> *** I answered this question based on the fact advertising was cancelled early that year, and more revenue would have been generated if that had continued.

ATTORNEY 2: Objection, compound question.
Q. (By ATTORNEY 2) Why?

A. Because those are customers that are existing and would have taken ***** anyway.
Q. No, I'm presupposing they did.
A. Uh-huh.
Q. So if more customers took ***** in 2015 than 2014, do you still believe the business was worth less at the end of 2015 than it was at the end of 2014?
A. Yes.
Q. So even though during G's unilateral operation of the business, if we presuppose more ***** than ever before, more customers than ever before, and more revenue than ever before, you're still telling me the value of the business went down?
ATTORNEY 1: Objection to –
THE WITNESS: I do not have –

> ***We had built up a customer base over several years it would make sense more **** were taken in that year.

ATTORNEY 1: – the form of the question -
THE WITNESS: – enough information to answer -
ATTORNEY 1: – as compound.
THE WITNESS: – that question.
Q. (By ATTORNEY 2) Are there any other losses you believe you sustained that you haven't told me -haven't told me about?
A. None that I can recall at this time.
Q. Is there a difference in your mind between future income and lost income? Because you identify them as two different components of damages. What's the difference, if any, between future income and lost income?

A. Future income to me is what I would have made if the business was running at the capacity that it was closed and with the same amount of growth and the income that would have been generated in the future. Could you please repeat the question.

Q. Sure. I'm asking you the difference in your mind between future income and lost income.

A. And lost income is what we would have lost -what we have lost by not advertising and by the business being closed.

> ***I should have not answered two questions at the same time. I should have clearly taken one at a time, but I just wanted this over.

Q. So am I understanding you correctly to assume that lost income is already past and future income is prospective? Is that the distinction you're drawing?

A. Without looking at how we did it on those papers, yes.

Q. And what do you understand the lost income to be? Because I think you were telling me the **** to *** is future income.

A. No, sir.

Q. That's total lost and future?

> ***He continually kept presenting answers, and not really asking a clear question.

A. I told you there's different components to that amount that we came to that would be also including starting the business back up and having it where it was at today.

Q. So that is the number of everything?

A. That – that – there's an increased cost to getting that done today.
Q. And who do you believe has knowledge of that increased cost that supports your position?
A. C*..
Q. Anyone else?
A. No.
ATTORNEY 2: I think I'm finished. Let's just take a quick break here and let me make certain, okay. (Recess taken at 4:10 p.m. to 4:15 p.m.)
Q. (By ATTORNEY 2) All right. One last thing. The pieces or components of your estimates of damages, do you have a recollection of what the cost is to restart the business?
A. I do not recall that figure without having it in front of me at this time.

> ***I did not have that figure. It was being worked on, and had not been presented yet. I did not want to say that. Everything in my case was being pushed to the wire.

Q. So now I am presupposing you restart the business on your own. Do you believe that to be more than some minimal or nominal sum?
ATTORNEY 1: Objection.
Q. (By ATTORNEY 2) More than five thousand dollars, for example?

> *** Here we go again, back and forth. I was not going to guess on this number. I did not have that number set in stone.

A. That sort of is based on whether or not the *** would be – would approve me, is the first biggest hurdle.
Q. So when you and H started –

> ***Even he was getting confused after this long day. At least I was still trying to pay attention.

A. G.
Q. When you and G started "My Business", what did it cost you to do so in time and in money?
A. The costs back then were way different seven years ago than they are today.
Q. What's different?
A. The optimization processes are different. Even M. has kind of alluded to the fact that they're different. Search engine is different. I can only go by what the experts are telling me. I don't have knowledge of anything other than what they're telling me.
Q. Okay. But you agree that you and G put up a *** dollars each and never put more money into the company?
A. I do not recall the numbers, total numbers, of what the business cost us out of pocket. I do not recall that at this time.

> ***This was over seven years ago. I did not have the exact figure, and was not going to guess.

Q. Did you ever put more money in after your thousand dollar initial contribution?
A. The initial contribution wasn't put in there all at one time.
Q. Regardless, you put in a thousand dollars, right? You already told me that. Did you ever put in more than that?

A. I do not recall.

> ***I was not sure where he was going with that number, that money would never have been touched. I was not going to expand on that answer.

Q. But today you think that number is a rather significant number?
A. It's a larger number.
ATTORNEY 1: I'm sorry, objection.
Q. (By ATTORNEY 2) Do you think it's like more than 50,000 dollars?
A. I do not recall the number that was given at the – given.
ATTORNEY 2: I don't have anything further. Thank you.
ATTORNEY 1: We're done. · (Deposition concluded at 4:17 p.m.)

Please be advised that I have read the foregoing deposition. I hereby state that there are: (check one)

_____ NO CORRECTIONS

_____ CORRECTIONS ATTACHED

_____

H

_____

Date Signed

Case Title: · v G
Date of Deposition: ·January 5, 2017
Job No: · · ·46400LR

—oOo—

B Kuffel

DEPONENT'S CHANGES OR CORRECTIONS

Note: If you are adding to your testimony, print the exact words you want to add. If you are deleting from your testimony, print the exact words you want to delete. Specify with "Add" or "Delete" and sign this form.

DEPOSITION OF: H
CASE: v G
DATE OF DEPOSITION: January 5, 2017

I, _____, have the following corrections to make to my deposition:

PAGE   LINE   ADD/CHANGE/DELETE

____   ____   _____
____   ____   _____
____   ____   _____
____   ____   _____
____   ____   _____
____   ____   _____
____   ____   _____
____   ____   _____
____   ____   _____
____   ____   _____
____   ____   _____
____   ____   _____
____   ____   _____
____   ____   _____

SIGNATURE_____ DATE_____

REPORTER'S CERTIFICATE

I certify that the foregoing proceedings in the within-entitled cause were reported at the time and place therein named; that said proceedings were reported by me, a duly Certified Shorthand Reporter of the State of California, and were thereafter transcribed into typewriting. I further certify that I am not of counsel or attorney for either or any of the parties to said cause of action, nor in any way interested in the outcome of the cause named in said cause of action. IN WITNESS WHEREOF, I have hereunto set my hand this 9th day of January, 2017.

***Recorders signature

*****, CSR No. ****
Certified Shorthand Reporter
For the State of California

B Kuffel

******* LEGAL SERVICES
The recorders address
*****, California *****
Phone number

January 9, 2017
H c/o Attorney 1's address.
******, California· ****

Re: v G
Date Taken: January 5, 2017

Dear Ms. :

Your deposition is now ready for you to read, correct, and sign. The original will be held in our office for 35 days from the date of this letter.

If you are represented by counsel, you may wish to discuss with him/her the reading and signing of your deposition. If your attorney has purchased a copy of your deposition, you may review that copy. If you choose to read your attorney's copy, please fill out, sign, and submit to our office the DEPONENT'S CHANGES OR CORRECTIONS page located in the back of your deposition.

If you choose to read your deposition at our office, it will be available between 9:00 a.m. and 4:00 p.m. Please bring this letter as a reference.

If you do not wish to read your deposition, please sign below and return within 35 days of the date of this letter.

_____   _____
H   DATE

Sincerely,
Recorder, CSR No. ***

***** Legal Services
Job No. *****cc. All Counsel
****** LEGAL SERVICES
Address
******, California· ******
Phone Number

Law Offices of Attorney #2
Address********, California· *****

Re: v G
Deposition of: H
Date Taken: January 5, 2017

Dear Attorney 2:

We wish to inform you of the disposition of this original transcript. The following procedure is being taken by our office:

_____ The witness has read and signed the ·deposition. (See attached)
_____ The witness has waived signature.
_____ The time for reading and signing has expired.
_____ The sealed original deposition is being forwarded to your office.
_____ Other:

Sincerely,

***** Legal Services
Ref. No. *****

**** I never saw my deposition prior to trial, it happened too close to court. I could not have ever corrected this mess and had it ready before court. I had no idea what to expect and what the questions were going to be asked, and I had no idea how long seven hours would become. This is an extremely stressful process.

I never had the chance to sit down and discuss my deposition with my attorney. We had only taken a few minutes after deposition to talk about it. He said this was a tough deposition, and he felt I did OK. He said no one walks away from a deposition unscathed.

There is also a cost to go back and talk about it and it would take hours. Even though I would love to go back and see what his thoughts were looking at it. That money will be spent elsewhere. This whole process is expensive, collecting, and reviewing interrogatories and using them for deposition. It is tens of thousands of dollars to get up to the point of deposition.

I hope this information helps someone else prepare for this process; I would have liked to have seen something like this before I had stepped through that door. It's your deposition and you have to do what is best for you. I wish you the best of luck, you will need it.

www.ingramcontent.com/pod-product-compliance
Lightning Source LLC
Chambersburg PA
CBHW031609210526
45464CB00004B/1498